BREAKUP

WHY THE WEST FEELS LEFT OUT OF CANADA

DON BRAID & SYDNEY SHARPE

KEY PORTER BOOKS

To the Spirit of the West —
Norma Osgood Sharpe and her grandchildren,
Gabriel Cardenas Braid and Rielle Braid

Canadian Cataloguing in Publication Data

Braid, Don, 1942-
Breakup

ISBN 1-55013-256-3

1. Federal-provincial relations – Canada.*
2. Canada – Politics and government – 1980-1984.*
3. Canada – Politics and government – 1984- .*
4. Canada, Western – Politics and government.

I. Sharpe, Sydney. II. Title.

FC630.B72 1990 971.064 C90-093715-7
F1034.2.B72 1990

Key Porter Books Limited
70 The Esplanade
Toronto, Ontario
M5E 1R2

Typesetting: Pixel Graphics

Printed on acid-free paper
Printed and bound in Canada
by T.H. Best Printing Company Limited

90 91 92 93 94 95 6 5 4 3 2 1

Contents

Acknowledgments

An enterprise like this book rests on many crucial pillars; take any one away, and the whole thing might collapse. Luckily, our pillars stayed firmly beneath us for many months, providing every kind of support – intellectual, moral and emotional. Only a few can be named here, but we sincerely thank them all.

Our children, Gabriel and Rielle, with the wisdom of youth, displayed endless patience as their parents toiled late into many nights. Norma Sharpe, with her western warmth and vitality, eased many a crisis as we tried to put some of her dreams into words. Thanks, too, to Hugh and Helen Braid, for their unflagging support. David Jones and Anne de Villars gave us sound constitutional advice and cheerful encouragement, as well as the use of that indispensable modern tool, the fax machine. Jack and Jenny Tulip, good neighbours, provided technical help at the eleventh hour. Jeff Dubois offered a stream of helpful suggestions along with unfailing friendship.

Dozens of politicians submitted to interviews for the book. We are sincerely grateful, but won't embarrass them by naming them here.

Many academics at the University of Alberta helped immensely; Dr. Peter Meekison, Dr. John Foster, Ms. Cathy Cavanaugh, Dr. Kenneth Norrie, Dr. Ted Chambers, Dr. Mike Percy and several others. They helped to shape the book's intellectual framework, although we accept complete responsibility for the interpretations.

Various libraries were invaluable, including the Library of Parliament in Ottawa, the University of Alberta Library and especially the Alberta Legislature Library, with its unfailingly helpful and friendly staff.

Ian Tyson graciously granted permission to quote from the lyrics of his songs: "Old Alberta Moon" © 1983 Speckled Bird Music, Capac; "Four Strong Winds" © 1986 Warner Bros. Music; "Rockies Twin Rose" © 1986 Slick Fork Music, Capac; "Since the Rain" © 1988 Slick Fork Music, Capac. The Star Phoenix granted permission to reprint the column by Les MacPherson.

We must recognize our endlessly patient editors at Key Porter Books, and book editor Margaret Allen, who suggested many improvements.

Finally, the book could not have been written without the forbearance and generosity of various colleagues at the Calgary Herald; publisher Kevin Peterson, former managing editor Gillian Steward, managing editor Crosbie Cotton, editors Susan Ruttan and Susan Scott, and bureau mates Jim Cunningham and Ashley Geddes. Their faith in the book often kept us going at difficult moments.

Any book like this springs from a wealth of friendships, conversations and experiences over many years. We believe it expresses our faith in the future of the West, and our passionate hope that all Canada will at last recognize the West as a full partner in Confederation.

INTRODUCTION

Bulldoze the Border

BREAKUP. WESTERN CANADA TREMBLES AT THE prospect. Westerners feel a thousand tremors shake their sense of loyalty to Canada, their bond to the nation, their age-old hope that the country can work for them. They talk openly about other options and solutions, but nobody seems to notice or care very much. Central Canada, as usual, focuses on its own ancient demons of language and unity, and the West, like any neglected partner, quietly prepares its mind for divorce.

Hardly anybody in the West wants to separate from Canada by an act of political will; in fact, support for western separatism is far smaller than it was in 1981 and 1982. Instead, westerners talk of a gradual, almost imperceptible trend to economic union with the United States – a much more likely outcome because it's so difficult to fight. Some westerners discuss this possibility with dread, but others embrace it eagerly. Free trade began this process, and federal neglect of the West accelerates it every day. Official Ottawa refuses to take seriously the plea for structural changes that would at last make westerners full partners in Confederation, and federal politicians rarely admit the existence of a problem at all. While they tinker, westerners slide farther into surly disaffection with the whole idea of Canada. Every tremor, each small crack in the foundation, makes it harder for concerned westerners to speak for their country.

Listen to Jeff Dubois, a sensitive man, a western francophone, a businessman and three-time candidate for the Alberta NDP, talk about the country he once defended passionately against all criticism: "Damn it, I'm fed up. This country's finished. Every time anybody with a bit of entrepreneurial spirit tries to do anything, they jack up the interest rates because they've got a problem in Toronto. It's wrecking the West. I'm ready to just pack it in and move to the States."

Listen to Mel Couvelier, British Columbia's straight-talking finance minister, who often speaks more directly than other western politicians: "On a straight dollars-and-cents basis, it doesn't make any sense for British Columbia to be in Confederation." Couvelier had good reason to be pessimistic. Just before he made the remark at a Vancouver conference in April 1990, he had been forced to rewrite the province's entire budget because of provisions in Michael Wilson's federal budget.

Listen to Saskatchewan premier Grant Devine, who said in a 1989 interview with one of the authors, while defending the Meech Lake accord: "If Quebec isn't part of the constitution, ten or fifteen years from now the province might drift away into independence. Then the West would be at risk because of much stronger economic ties with the Americans, through free trade. It would then be very easy to join the Americans." Devine made the comment even though he was one of the West's most ardent boosters of free trade. The collapse of the Meech Lake accord in June 1990 makes his prediction even more credible.

To many westerners, relations with the United States often seem friendlier, more productive, and less complicated than dealings with Central Canada. Chris Watts, an advisor in the office of Premier Bill Vander Zalm, told the April 1990 Vancouver conference that free trade is pushing the countries closer together. "In the passage of time, I believe it will emulate the European experience of a common market," he said. The subject of the conference – regional economic integration – was itself ominous to any Canadian nationalist.

All this is being noticed in the United States, where the scent of Canadian blood always whets expansionist appetites. Patrick Buchanan, a right-wing columnist for the *Washington Times*, expressed the century-old American dream of Manifest Destiny when he wrote: "There is nothing wrong with Americans dreaming of a republic which, by the year 2000, encompasses the Maritime and western provinces of Canada, Yukon and Northwest Territories all the way to the Pole, and contains the world's largest island, Greenland, purchased from Denmark, giving the United States a land mass rivaling that of the U.S.S.R., under a constitution permitting all her people to realize their dreams."

Appalling as this vision might be to Canadians, one point is true: the U.S. Constitution does allow all its regions to realize their dreams, and the Canadian Constitution does not. As a result, almost all Americans love their constitution, while many western Canadians mistrust theirs and even fear it. Until this crucial defect is repaired, the West will never be secure in Canada and the American dream will always be appealing to many westerners.

British Columbia is already embarked on a happy spurt of

economic co-operation with Oregon and Washington State to the south. Evoking the image of the Berlin Wall, Seattle developer Paul Schell told the Vancouver meeting: "Bulldoze the border. Keep the Peace Arch, demolish the rest and send the pieces to our friends around the world." Nobody ran him out of the province or even jumped to Canada's defence.

Westerners would not consider such thoughts if they felt comfortable within Canada. But always, it seems, somebody else's concerns come first. Quebec's constitutional problems are an eternal federal obsession. During the exhausting Meech Lake debate, westerners heard constantly that they would wreck the country if they didn't support the accord. But federal politicians didn't see any harm to the nation in delaying western demands for Senate reform. Once again, westerners felt that their concerns and solutions were not considered legitimate by Ottawa and Central Canada.

When westerners are allowed to stop thinking about Quebec, they are forced to ponder Ontario, the province that controls their economic lives. The smallest twitch of the Ontario economy makes the Bank of Canada snap to attention. When inflation went up a notch in late 1989, the bank responded with higher interest rates that slowed recovery across the West, where inflation was far lower. This happened even though the western premiers had been pleading with the bank for two years to consider the whole country, not just Ontario. The premiers even sent Premier Devine to talk to the bank's governor, John Crow. It did no good. The rates rose inexorably, slowly strangling vibrant economies in Alberta and British Columbia. As usual, westerners could only fume – and notice that interest rates were several points lower in the United States. A western businessman summed up a typical western perception: "When Ontario does well, we do badly. When Ontario does badly, we do badly."

Ontario's dominance wouldn't be so hard to take if the province were more sensitive. But westerners can't help noticing the peculiar mixture of paternalism and unintended ignorance that often marks Ontario's dealings with the West. This attitude can show in little things: the Ontario business contact who calls Vancouver at 5:00 a.m. and says, "Hey, sorry, I didn't know it was so early out there"; or the Torontonian's amazement when he learns that Edmonton has sixteen live theatres. More seriously, it shows up in the smug belief of Ontario politicians that they speak for all English Canada and that Ontarians truly care about the nation, while others are self-interested regionalists. Most of all, westerners resent having their opinions dismissed as crackpot because they aren't necessarily what Ontario wants to hear.

These opinions vary across the West, of course, because the region is diverse and complex. The four provinces have vastly different histories, political cultures and emotional climates. Manitoba, being in the geographic centre of Canada, and closest to Ontario, tends to be the most centralist. But its special problems, especially when language is involved, can turn the province quickly against Ottawa. Saskatchewan is the gentlest and perhaps the most civilized of the western provinces, the least severe in its reactions, but still profoundly alienated from the federal system. Albertans are usually the angriest westerners because they believe they have been robbed blind by Confederation. British Columbians, secure and often oblivious in their glorious world beyond the mountains, are linked to Canada by the most fragile bonds of any province except Quebec. Obviously, these statements are large generalizations; some Albertans don't feel wronged at all, and many British Columbians are passionately devoted to Canada. But the prevailing views in each province shape the way it deals with the country. Nobody who reads the newspapers or watches TV can doubt that when westerners feel wronged by Canada, they react with hostility that unites them from Winnipeg to

Victoria in what one political scientist called "a region of the mind." The very depth of their anger shows that they still care about the country, but more and more, they also express indifference, dismissal or disgust. Those are the truly dangerous emotions – the cold ones that can lead to breakup.

The problems go far beyond the abilities of any government to solve through tinkering or fiddling. They are rooted in the deepest structure of the country. Canada is a badly built nation – the only democratic federation in the western world in which every important institution, from the Supreme Court to the Senate, is dominated by the population centres. The largest provinces enjoy a multiple majority that spills into every level of federal government. They control the House of Commons, as they should, but they also provide 6 of 9 Supreme Court judges, 48 of 104 senators, and most members of federal boards and commissions. The second-largest country in the world simply can't work that way. Every other successful federation, from Australia to the United States and Switzerland, recognizes some form of regional equality to balance the power of population. But Canada, with its clumsy colonial past, regards the idea as vaguely radical, just another crazy western notion.

Canada can stumble along with the current system, maybe for a few decades, perhaps indefinitely. But the country will never reach anything like its true potential, and ultimately it will fail. Westerners are beginning to sense this in their bones. Their great problem, the one they've always had, is to make the national leaders listen and penetrate the indifference of Central Canada. The authors hope this book will provide a modest start, by explaining why westerners feel the way they do and how some of the problems might be solved.

Many of the perceptions here are shaped partly by experience in Alberta, where the authors live and work. But the ideas apply equally to the whole region and to the country itself. A great western idea – the belief in regional equality – began in Alberta and is now spreading quickly across the region. If Canada accepts this idea and builds it into the central system, the West could at last be a contented partner in Confederation. But if the idea is ignored or brushed aside, the West will slide farther away from the national system. The breakup that federal politicians dread so much might begin not with the noisy departure of Quebec out the front door, but with the slow, quiet withdrawal of the West through the servants' entrance at the back.

There is time to act. Westerners still love the idea of Canada and hope the country can some day work to everyone's full benefit. The region is more mature and confident than it has ever been, better able to resist small shocks and disappointments. More than anything else, westerners long to be turned loose as equals, so they can use their energies for the good of their region and all Canada. But they feel held back, reined in, by a national system that was not created with their needs in mind. If this feeling persists, the energy will sooner or later be directed somewhere else.

Canada has a choice to make: it can continue to muddle along with a bad system, and perhaps lose the whole country, or it can listen to western ideas and build a great nation.

ONE

The West Wants In

PITY THE FEDERAL GOVERNMENTS, FOR IN WESTERN Canada they can never be heroes for long. Most governments are popular for a while, but after a few years, usually about one term in office, westerners revert to their usual suspicion and contempt. The great western journalist Bob Edwards expressed this feeling with wicked accuracy when he wrote in the *Calgary Eye Opener* in 1918: "Probably the saddest thing about Ottawa is the number of fourth-rate intellects applied to first-rate problems." Westerners have always felt that Ottawa doesn't care about their problems, and that, in the brief periods when it does, it lacks the brains to solve them. Like a backward student, the federal government has a short attention span for the West; a cry for help from Ontario or Quebec always catches its ear and sends it rushing off in another direction. The politicians often do their best, or try to, but they know where their masters are. In a system as lopsided as Canada's, they have no choice but to obey the provinces with the most voters. Westerners understand this with absolute clarity, but western members of federal governments keep trying to convince them that things have changed, that the West is equal at last. They always fail.

In his fifteenth-floor office in Edmonton's federal building, Don Mazankowski is puzzled and a bit confused as 1989 draws to a close. The deputy prime minister – Western Canada's most powerful federal politician – believes his government is a true friend of the West. Mazankowski, an imposing, intense politician with a cart-horse appetite for work, is doing his best, and he definitely is not a fourth-rate intellect. But down below on Jasper Avenue, and far beyond the vast horizons that stretch away to Saskatchewan and British Columbia, the voters are angry. They have almost always been angry at Ottawa for more than a hundred years, but now they seem to be building toward one of the blind rages that come every decade or so. The last one was in 1980, when the Liberals introduced the National Energy Program. The new anti-Tory rage is sparked by the goods and services tax (GST), patronage, the Meech Lake accord, crooks in the Tory caucus, animosity toward Quebec, and other irritants large and small. Mazankowski, an Albertan from Vegreville, finds himself in the strange spot of defending a prime minister almost as unpopular with westerners as Pierre Trudeau was ten years earlier. In a way this is even worse; westerners respected Trudeau through their hatred, but they have little regard for Brian Mulroney, whom they brand with contemptuous insults – liar, cheat, hypocrite.

In Alberta and B.C., furious westerners flock to Reform Party of Canada meetings, demanding that Ottawa junk the Meech Lake deal, get tough with Quebec and balance the budget. Everywhere in the region, rallies against the GST draw large, nasty crowds. One of Mazankowski's Alberta colleagues in the Conservative caucus, Edmonton Southeast MP David Kilgour, says publicly that his own party treats the West badly because the prime minister doesn't care. Within three months Kilgour and Calgary Northeast MP, Dr. Alex Kindy, will be booted out of the Tory caucus for their opposition to the GST, and both will come home to a hero's welcome.

It's just after Christmas and the bargain hunters are bustling in the streets, but Mazankowski feels no holiday spirit, finds his job no special bargain. Some days he almost wishes he were back in Opposition so he could criticize without having to act. That's what Kilgour is doing, Mazankowski suggests with a mixture of bitterness and nostalgia. It's an easier life, even though you can't actually accomplish anything.

He has some cause to be puzzled, because by many standards the Tories should be much more popular in the West than they are. Even Mazankowski's office is a sign of how hard they are trying. The furnishings are almost spartan – a basic desk, sofa, chair and table. If Mazankowski were at the same level in the private sector, his secretary would have this room. And it isn't even his, not really. He shares the office when he's in town with Dr. Bruce Rawson, the deputy minister in charge of the Western Diversification Initiative (WDI). External Affairs Minister Joe Clark uses it when he needs to be close to his Yellowhead riding west of Edmonton. The only reason the Alberta capital even has this office (and the headquarters of the whole WDI) is because of Mazankowski's massive clout in cabinet.

The austere office is a perfect reflection, in fact, of the pressures the government faces in the West. On one hand, Mazankowski says, westerners want federal spending to make up for many years of neglect. On the other, they insist that the government cut waste and reduce the deficit. "We get mixed signals," he says, vastly understating the government's western dilemma. "We started out in 1984 in an attempt to scale down government spending. We were clobbered. There was a sense that just as the West was about to get its due, you guys are going to cut back. And we did. We went through that, and came out with the GST, and now we're hammered with the charge that we're spending too much money. As politicians we're somewhat exasperated.... It's not getting any easier."

Even as they cut, slashing away at tired institutions like Via Rail, the Tories delivered the WDI. It's exactly the kind of thing westerners have wanted for decades – a program of federal aid to businesses, issued mainly as repayable loans. It tends to favour small aggressive firms with new ideas in technology, the kind of enterprise that might end reliance on resources. Across the region, money and advice are pouring into computer firms, processing companies – even a family firm in Medicine Hat that makes fold-down tables for changing diapers. By the end of 1989, the WDI, and other programs relating to the West, had signed deals worth $665.4 million with 1,289 projects. As far as anybody knew, there was no money for boondoggles like the famous federal loans to strip clubs near bureaucrats' offices in Hull, Quebec. Most westerners who deal with WDI find it quick, efficient and responsive – for a government agency, at least (although it was spending a fair bit on administration – $63 million in salaries for 320 civil servants over three years). Mazankowski has the influence to get things done, and he decided early that the WDI was going to work, not bog down in red tape.

Besides the WDI, there was more than $20 billion in farm aid over several years, and a growing volume of federal purchasing from western companies. The biggest was a $380 million Transport Department contract with Hughes Aircraft of Canada, newly headquartered in Calgary, to build a computerized air-traffic control system for the nation. More than 80 per cent of the work would be done in the West, said Transport Minister Benoît Bouchard.

These are genuine efforts to address the old western feeling that all the federal goodies go to Ontario and Quebec. The trend is so obvious that David Peterson, the Ontario Liberal premier, says almost plaintively: "We don't get any breaks out of the federal government, there's no question about that. I guess there's a sense from them that we're doing okay, we don't need any help. The federal government is highly partisan, it's unbelievably partisan." (Peterson might be right about partisanship, but he neglects to mention that Ottawa has a program much like the WDI for underdeveloped Northern Ontario.)

In the past, a juicy contract like the one awarded to Hughes would have gone automatically to Toronto or Montreal. But the announcement of this bonanza had very little impact in the West, changed few minds from their fixed notion that Ottawa is unfair, biased, crooked, always a servant of Ontario and Quebec. Given the choice, the average westerner will ignore breakthroughs like the Hughes contract to fume about the 1986 decision to give the CF-18 jet fighter maintenance contract to Montreal rather than to Winnipeg (a move that was certainly unfair and biased). Western grievance, so deeply rooted in history, doesn't turn its head easily to the present. Sometimes Mazankowski and other Tories feel as if all the money and good intentions are sinking without a bubble in the vast sea of western hostility.

They can't do much about it, says the deputy prime minister. If the Conservatives trumpet their western spending, they're branded as wastrels by many of the same people who want the West to get its share. Mazankowski had just met with Edmonton businessmen, solid Tories, who were looking for a piece of federal programs. Such people are unpredictable, he suggests; the next day they might argue that the Via cutbacks hurt western tourism, and then launch into a tirade about the federal deficit. The West is never as uncomplicated as it appears from the outside, but these days it seems even more perplexing than ever, a jumble of contradictions that spell nightmare for politicians like Mazankowski.

He complains, with some cause, that the media are encouraging old stereotypes instead of focusing on what happens today. "When an announcement for Quebec is made," he says, "it is usually highlighted in the western media. When something for the West comes up, it sure as heck is highlighted in the Quebec press.... There's a certain tendency for Quebec journalists to fan the fires of animosity between Quebec and the rest of Canada, and I think the same thing applies in Western Canada.... It's that kind of feeling that leads to the tension." Mazankowski has a point; for instance, there was probably more coverage in the West of the decision to move a federal prison to Mulroney's riding than there has been for the whole Western Diversification program.

Mazankowski will keep working and trying. He never stops. "I can't stomach his ideology, but I have to give him credit for going flat out and doing the best he can," says a former constituent in his Vegreville riding. But even if the government plopped the entire federal budget into Western Canada, the suspicion wouldn't end. Western mistrust of Ottawa is built into Canadian history and the national system. History can't change, and until the system does, the West will likely follow its old pattern of taking from the federal government with one hand and smacking it contemptuously with the other. Another of Bob Edwards's journalistic floggings, administered in 1906, sounds to westerners as if it were written in 1990: "The history of the Conservative party in western Canada for the past 10 years has been one long, continuous blunder. They have done every damned thing they ought not to have done, and haven't done a single thing any sane man might be expected to do."

The resentments that power western alienation endure

and always find expression somewhere – through the Reform Party one year, through a true separatist party the next, through the right wing of the Tory party in milder times, just as often through the NDP in Manitoba, Saskatchewan and British Columbia. Whenever things turn sour for a Don Mazankowski, whenever a Brian Mulroney is booed or a Joe Clark is accused of betraying the West, the underlying reasons are always the same – westerners believe the country isn't fair. Until it is, they will scold and fume at Ottawa and generally make pests of themselves. This is what colonials do best, and westerners are very good at it. History has taught them well.

Stereotypes of the angry westerner are burned into the national psyche. There's the old image of the wheat farmer who, after a long summer without rain, shakes his fist at the empty sky and rages: "God damn the CPR!" Another farmer, asked what he would do with a million dollars just won in the lottery, is supposed to have said: "I'll just keep planting crops until it's all gone." Harry Strom, the Socred premier of Alberta from 1968 to 1971, caught the same feeling when he remarked in 1970: "We have always had a sense of economic exploitation. This notion has marked all political parties in the West. The cartoon that has captured these sentiments is one of a large cow standing on a map of Canada, munching grass in Alberta and Saskatchewan with milk pouring from a bulging udder into the large buckets of Ontario."

Westerners have been debating the causes of these attitudes for more than a century. The usual suspects are Ottawa and the national political system created at Confederation, but some westerners doubt there are any real villains in the piece. Kenneth Norrie, a University of Alberta economist, argues that the West is a victim of small population, distance from markets, and a boom-or-bust resource economy. Tariffs were in place before settlement began, and immigrants should have calculated for this, Norrie says. In other words, the western deal was clear from the start, and those who didn't like it weren't forced to live with it.

Critics counter that immigrants were bombarded in their homelands with Canadian government propaganda showing a rich, bountiful and completely mythical life on the frontier. Even the artistic techniques were extremely devious; posters ignored the emptiness and vast skies of the prairies, focusing instead on busy, plentiful fields and foregrounds. Ducks looked as fat and juicy as turkeys, cattle as big as boxcars. One poster showed a beautiful woman in angel-like robes sailing over farmsteads, scattering wheat from a basket to the fields below. Some of the scenes look suspiciously like the European countries the propaganda was aimed at. Many immigrants attracted by this misleading advertising jumped at free homesteads, but had no idea they were heading into a primitive, remote and difficult land where they would have no political or economic clout.

Still, Norrie maintains that the disadvantages to living in the West were not unfair in the national context. With the best will in the world, Ottawa couldn't do much to correct this fundamental economic problem, he argues. His theory has been treated seriously even by western Canadian scholars with a bias against Ottawa. Some point out that in the days when Manitoba, Saskatchewan and Alberta didn't control their resources and public lands, the federal government compensated the provinces with a yearly subsidy. These subsidies, however, were never enough to cover the local demand for services.

By international standards, the West can hardly claim to be oppressed at all; this is not South Africa or the Soviet Union. There are many ugly episodes in western history (the murder of Louis Riel, the brutal crushing of the Winnipeg General Strike in 1919, the systematic removal of Indians from their lands to unproductive reservations), but nothing that approaches, say, the enslavement of American blacks or Britain's treatment of Ireland. Natives have good reason to disagree, but their legitimate feeling of physical occupation and oppression is not shared by the majority of westerners. The West is not held by force and westerners are not denied any fundamental rights enjoyed by other Canadians. They have never been angry enough at the national system to boycott it; despite their flirtations with separatism, they keep sending MPS to Ottawa. Beneath all the anger and cynicism lies a persistent faith in the idea of Canada, a belief that the country can be made to work. The brilliant Reform Party slogan – "The West Wants In" – is the best four-word description ever penned of the western attitude over 150 years.

Undeniably, though, westerners are disappointed by their standing in Canada. Often they don't believe they are treated as the political equals of Canadians in other provinces. National treatment of the region, they feel, is not worthy of Canada's high standards and ideals. They sense that they have always been kept in the waiting room of national life, never to be admitted to the main chamber because others don't want them in. This feeling is so strong, argues Roger Gibbons, a political scientist at the University of Calgary, that it amounts to a "political ideology of regional discontent." It binds very different provinces and people in a kind of "region of the mind." Manitoba often has centralist leanings, but when an unfriendly federal decision hits, the province explodes in a purely western fury. Saskatchewan and Alberta, with their vastly different political cultures, march to the same drum if their resources are threatened. British Columbia can seem to lie sleepily for years, yet it almost always rises with the Prairies in pitched battles against federal power. Across the region, Gibbons says, "there is great continuity with the past, continuity expressed through the interlocking themes that Western Canada is always outgunned in national politics and that, as a consequence, it has been subjected to varying degrees of economic exploitation by Central Canada.... In the eyes of the alienated westerner, systematic and predictable political patterns are clearly discernible; the West consistently gets shortchanged, exploited and ripped off." Goodwill and faith will not endure forever against such dangerous perceptions.

The trouble started at the very beginning, when the Prairie West was purchased by Canada, and then treated as a possession through all the stages of its slow, painful and incomplete integration into the nation. Much of this strange history is often forgotten even by Western Canadians – or never learned. School texts, printed mainly in Ontario and focusing on "national" history, largely ignore the roots of western protest. Yet history explains everything about modern tensions between the West and Ottawa.

For two hundred years, the Hudson's Bay Company (HBC) owned the vast territory that now includes Alberta, Saskatchewan and Manitoba. The absentee landlord in London saw this huge domain in purely commercial terms: it supplied fur for the British and European markets, in return for payments in cash and kind (usually as little as possible) to native fur harvesters. The North West Company, called the Nor'Westers, controlled by Montreal traders, threatened this dominance by pushing north through the Athabasca region to the Arctic and the Pacific, opening rich new areas to the fur trade. The competition between them was brutal, sometimes bloody, and too costly to continue. In 1821 the two companies merged into an even larger Hudson's Bay Company. The western population reflected all this international action; besides the many groups of western Indians, there were "French-speaking Métis, English-speaking half-breeds, officers and men of the Hudson's Bay Company, Selkirk settlers, a handful of missionaries, retired soldiers, and free traders," writes Donald Swainson in *Canada Annexes the*

West. Most of these people were centred around the forks of the Red and Assiniboine rivers in what is now Manitoba. "This was a civilized society, with its own churches, schools and law courts." But "a willingness to resist in spite of dependence and relative weakness was a striking western characteristic long before the West was annexed by Canada," Swainson says. "It is an important component of the western context of federalism."

By 1869, the Confederation of Ontario, Quebec, Nova Scotia, and New Brunswick allowed for the later inclusion of the North-West Territories and Rupert's Land. The United States had just bought Alaska from the Russians. Free trade was thriving between St. Paul and the Red River Settlement, and Minnesota had long sought the annexation of the British northwest. Confederation was in large part a defensive stand against American expansionism that emerged after the Civil War. Threatened from all sides, the Fathers of Confederation gave little thought to the political and democratic rights of western settlers. Canada was so highly centralized, in fact, that it hardly qualified as a federation at all. In one sense, Confederation simply transferred the British colonial system from London to Ottawa, along with all the colonial powers over trade, commerce and local self-government that Britain had always exercised. All the provinces soon began to fight this control in one way or another, but the Prairie West started with unique disadvantages.

In 1868, the new Dominion bought the Hudson's Bay Company's vast lands for a combination of money and vast tracts of territory – £300,000, one-twentieth of the arable land to be opened for settlement, and title to the land already held as trading posts. This made the HBC a major commercial player in the West (and a major annoyance to many westerners) for another century. Manitoba became a truncated province in 1870, and the rest of the vast territory was administered from Ottawa. The federal government regarded the new region as its possession, bought and paid for, whose sole purpose was to serve the strategic and commercial interests of the original partners in Confederation. There was plenty of romantic rhetoric about the new lands, especially the bunk aimed at immigrants, but the truth was the West was good for business.

As the prolific Canadian historian W.L. Morton has pointed out, the West was "annexed as a subordinate territory." Swainson adds: "Ontario's leaders were anxious that expansion take place quickly, and assumed that Ontarians would benefit through the creation of a miniature Ontario in the West." Clifford Sifton, the minister of the interior from 1896 to 1905, had a clear idea of the kind of western settler he wanted: "a stalwart peasant in a sheepskin coat, born on the soil, whose forefathers have been farmers for ten generations, with a stout wife and a half-dozen children." Historian D.J. Hall concludes: "What he wanted was peasant stock who could and would struggle through on their prairie farms, and who would be succeeded by their children and grandchildren on the same farms." But the West was not to be the equal of Sifton's own home in Anglo-Saxon western Ontario. In 1904, this powerful minister in the Laurier government articulated his vision of the region to an audience in Winnipeg:

> What will western Canada do for the Canadian organism? Sir, it will give a vast and profitable traffic to its railways and steamship lines. It will give remunerative employment to tens of thousands of men.... It will do more. It will build up our Canadian seaports.... It will furnish a steady and remunerative business to the manufacturers of eastern Canada, giving assured prosperity where uncertainty now exists. These are the things the west will do for the east.

Sifton made it absolutely clear that Western Canada was to supply resources for industry and seaports, and markets for manufactured goods. The West would be a support base for the larger national economy. Wilfrid Laurier himself spoke even more to the point in 1903. "The best way you can help the manufacturers of Canada," he said, "is to fill up the prairie regions of Manitoba and the Northwest with a prosperous and contented people who will be the consumers of the manufactured goods of the east".

In Centennial Year, 1967, W.L. Morton still detected this fundamental truth about Confederation. It was "brought about to increase the wealth of central Canada, and until that original purpose is altered, and the concentration of wealth and population by national policy in central Canada ceases, Confederation must remain an instrument of injustice."

The plain fact is that seven provinces entered Confederation as legal equals, but Manitoba, Saskatchewan and Alberta did not. Manitoba was a tiny "postage stamp" rectangle, comprising little more than the Red River Colony, when it joined Canada in 1870. Most important, even after Manitoba was allowed to expand to its present boundaries, it was deprived of control over its own lands and resources until 1930.

The province was created in the first place, historians note, only because the Macdonald government was forced into it by the first Riel Rebellion. This uprising was itself the result of federal failure to consider the needs of a proud settlement. In 1869, Ottawa enraged the Métis and white settlers by unilaterally sending a governor to preside over the newly purchased territory. The charismatic Métis leader Louis Riel and his allies responded by setting up a provisional government, and Ottawa was in no position to reply with military force. The Americans were hunting for an excuse to intervene, Britain was urging a peaceful settlement, and Quebec was bound to react angrily to an attack on Métis settlers. So the Dominion government negotiated the creation of Manitoba, with these assurances: French language rights, control of education, settlement of Métis land claims and representation in Ottawa. But as historian J.F. Conway observes in his fine survey, *The West: The History of a Region in Confederation*:

> The Dominion government made up for these humiliations in other ways, finally stealing by stealth what had been a significant victory for the Métis nation and their white allies . . . the size of Manitoba was tightly constricted to about 10,000 square miles, barely encompassing most of the settlement on the Red and Assiniboine rivers. It became known as the "postage stamp province" and was the subject of some hilarity among easterners. Alexander Mackenzie, leader of the Liberal Opposition, said, "The whole thing has such a ludicrous look that it only puts one in mind of some incidents in *Gulliver's Travels* . . . it is one of the most preposterous schemes . . . ever submitted to the legislature."

The denial of resource control, Conway adds, "made it impossible for the province to plan and influence settlement, to dispose of, and gain revenues from, timber resources, or, indeed, any resources that began to be developed."

Alberta and Saskatchewan were also denied this resource ownership when they became provinces in 1905. For the next twenty-five years, they were forced to wheedle, complain and threaten to get the same privileges that other provinces had always enjoyed (including British Columbia, which became a province in 1871, and Prince Edward Island, which joined in 1873). Even when the federal government no longer needed control of lands and minerals in order to encourage settlement, it refused to let go. Not until 1930 did Ottawa finally agree to transfer ownership under the Natural Resources Transfer Act. Fifty years later, when Ottawa tried to limit the rights of ownership through the National Energy Program, many westerners saw a familiar pattern. After all that time, amazingly, Ottawa still wasn't quite willing to recognize the Constitution. The explosion that followed was predictable to anybody who understood this crucial point of western history. It seemed that in Ottawa's eyes, western resources fell under different rules simply because of their location. As westerners told themselves time and again, "They wouldn't do this if the oil was in Ontario or Quebec." They were probably right.

Former Liberal cabinet minister Eric Kierans, reflecting on the oddness of the long delay in resource transfer, once explained that there was no other example in the British Empire of people being denied control of lands when they won a measure of self-government. "By British law and tradition," he wrote, "the ownership and control of the public domain was always handed over to the political authority designated by a community when the citizens assumed responsibility for the government of their own affairs."

But the Prairies were not really regarded as a community, and certainly not as potential equals within Canada. They were strategic connective tissue intended to bind the country together and hold off the ambitious Americans. Denied the revenue base they needed to pay for their own administration, the new provinces faced the constant humiliation of pleading cap in hand with Ottawa. Often the subsidies fell far short of the local demand for services, and this impeded provincial development. Those humbling years of colonial status created two attitudes, contradictory but understandable, that persist in the Prairies today: the urge to make up for lost years by squeezing as much out of Ottawa as possible; and the desire to be self-reliant so that no help is ever needed again.

British Columbia shares much of the Prairie resentment of Ottawa, but has a vastly different mentality because it was treated much more fairly at Confederation. The prosperous and desirable Crown colony was formed by the British government in 1866 through the union of Vancouver's Island and the mainland colony of British Columbia. The new colony was lured, courted and wooed into Canada in 1871 by John A. Macdonald's government with the promise of a railway and guaranteed ownership of resources and lands. British Columbia didn't join out of affection, as one of the colony's negotiators noted sharply in 1870. "The people of this Colony have, generally speaking, no love for Canada," wrote Dr. John Sebastian Helmcken. "Therefore no union on account of love need be looked for. The only bond of Union outside of force – and force the Dominion has not – will be the material advantage of the country and the pecuniary benefits of the inhabitants." That remains today a fair summary of the attitude of British Columbians. Conway sums up the vast difference between B.C. and the Prairies:

> The Prairie region entered Confederation as a colonial possession of the Dominion government. B.C. negotiated the terms of Confederation as a fully fledged British colony. This distinction is crucial and goes much of the way in explaining why B.C.'s relations with Central Canada have rarely been as tumultuous as the Prairies'. B.C. had to be wooed and won. The Prairies were simply purchased from absentee owners without consultation with the local people. B.C. seriously considered other options to Confederation. The Prairies were not permitted this luxury.

For these reasons, British Columbians are much more confident, more sure of their identity, more likely just to ignore the rest of the country for long stretches. Canada has to prove itself to them, they believe, while Prairie dwellers feel a burning need to prove themselves to Canada (although they rarely admit it.) The Prairie inferiority complex, branded into the region's psyche, is slow to fade. The Prairies are obsessed by Canada – by their role in the country, their striving to be equal, their near-paranoia that what they won will be taken away again. British Columbians are rarely so defensive. In the early 1970s, former premier Dave Barrett actually offered to share resource control with Ottawa. Any Prairie premier who did that would risk being lynched.

The West has always fought back in two predictable

ways: by creating its own political parties, both federal and provincial, to challenge "national" parties; and by trusting western premiers to fight Ottawa. Westerners invented the Progressive party, the United Farmers, Social Credit, the Co-operative Commonwealth Federation (CCF) (since 1961 the NDP), sent them off to do battle in the national capital, and just as often elected them as provincial governments as well. These parties, or odd mixtures of them, have run the western provinces for much of the past seventy years. In Manitoba, an alliance of the United Farmers of Manitoba and the Progressives ruled from 1922 to 1936; the Liberal-Progressives from 1936 to 1958; and the NDP from 1969 to 1977, and again from 1981 to 1988. In British Columbia, the Socreds swept to power in 1952, gave way to the NDP in 1972, and returned to office in 1975. Albertans elected the United Farmers in 1921, replaced them with Social Credit in 1935, then kept that remarkable party in office until 1971. Saskatchewan elected the CCF from 1944 to 1964, and its successor, the NDP, from 1971 to 1982.

Lately the trend is toward provincial government by "national" parties (the Tories in Manitoba, Saskatchewan and Alberta), but to hold office they are often forced to behave like third parties. The Alberta Conservatives, for instance, have no formal link with the federal party, and Premier Don Getty fights a nasty war of words over the sales tax. In Manitoba, Premier Gary Filmon has been one of the toughest critics of Meech Lake and federal language policy. Only Grant Devine in Saskatchewan has seemed relatively compliant, and this perception wounded him badly in the local opinion polls.

The need to resist Ottawa also pushes the western premiers to form some unlikely alliances among themselves. In 1986, former Manitoba premier Howard Pawley, a New Democrat, was so overcome by regional solidarity that he signed a western premiers' communiqué calling for a "common market" with the United States. Pawley then spent two years explaining to his party in Manitoba that he didn't really mean it. The other western premiers, all conservatives, snickered in private over this strange twist. The joke in Grande Prairie, where the meeting was held, was that they won Pawley's agreement by threatening to throw him overboard during a powerboat ride on the Peace River.

The most successful alliance of all came in 1973, when three New Democrats and a Tory lined up to thump Prime Minister Trudeau at the Western Economic Opportunities Conference held in Calgary. Trudeau agreed to this meeting because his party had dropped from twenty-six western seats to just seven in the 1972 election. He wanted to show the West that he cared, but federal officials seemed to believe they could divide and rule at the meeting. After all, nobody could reasonably expect a common front among Dave Barrett, Allan Blakeney and Ed Schreyer, the New Democrats, and Peter Lougheed, the Conservative. There was still a feeling that these premiers were rural hicks who couldn't match the subtle Ottawa mandarins. "They were going to dazzle us with their brilliance," recalls Gordon Young, then an assistant to Alberta's federal affairs minister, Don Getty. But the feds were not well prepared for the remarkable assault they faced under the hot glare of the national TV lights at Mount Royal College.

The premiers had done a good deal of phoning, meeting and plotting before the conference began. Where they couldn't agree – on energy policy, for instance – they simply left the matter off the agenda. (Lougheed claimed mischievously that they had done this out of fairness, because Ontario wasn't at the table.) Where they did find common ground, they argued detailed and well-researched opinions on everything from freight rates to farm machinery testing. Trudeau advanced the view that western alienation resulted largely from symbols and perception rather than real problems (although he conceded there were some of those, too). The premiers snapped back with dozens of examples of discrimination. "What we really want is to be a full part of the Canadian team," Lougheed said. "We would like to play a full role in Confederation and not feel held back." Blakeney, who always had the knack of rising above the prosaic, demanded that Ottawa "free our hands of the shackles of history."

Trudeau began to realize he was facing a determined bunch who had planned their attack, and he was not amused. The prime minister and the premiers even wrangled over who had the right to make opening statements on each issue. As the conference came to a close, Lougheed praised Trudeau effusively for his fairness, perhaps with tongue in cheek. When Trudeau banged down the final gavel, he snapped: "Well, thus ends the one – and only – Western Economic Opportunities Conference!" Trudeau has been proved right; the federal government hasn't taken a similar risk since. Gordon Young recalls proudly, "We were better prepared, and we creamed 'em."

From that moment in July 1973, the Liberals knew they faced some tough, determined people joined in an alliance of all four western provinces. The West was beginning to produce a coherent strategy, largely because, under Barrett, British Columbia became a regular participant at western premiers' conferences. (Barrett's predecessor, W.A.C. Bennett, had never shown much interest in joining the rather sleepy earlier gatherings of Prairie premiers, called the Prairie Economic Conference.) The meetings of the four premiers, rotated each year among small communities in the provinces, quickly became a rich lode of anti-Ottawa rhetoric and strategy. By the end of the 1970s, the angry premiers were preparing annual "intrusions lists," documents that detailed all the objectionable federal forays into provincial turf. At their silliest, these lists attacked the federal government for claiming authority over video games. In 1978 there were fifty-seven complaints, many of them equally petty. At their most effective, though, such tactics sent Ottawa a clear message that the West was united on resource ownership and other key issues.

During this whole period, Lougheed was infuriating federal mandarins and ministers with a campaign to raise the status of provincial governments in their dealings with Ottawa. His method was simple; he refused to talk to anybody but the prime minister, and his ministers dismissed anyone below their federal counterparts. "He was annoyed because of what had happened to his people," says Dr. Peter Meekison, who was then deputy minister of federal affairs in Lougheed's government. "After they were elected in 1971, the ministers would go eagerly down to Ottawa and get shuffled off to an assistant deputy minister. Not even a deputy, an assistant deputy! Lougheed decided he wouldn't stand for it." The premier broke his own rule only once when he met Trudeau's emissary on constitutional change, Gordon Robertson. "The federal people were quite upset by this, but they got used to it," says Meekison. Lougheed's move challenged Trudeau's central belief that Ottawa is always the senior government. But the premier made it stick and the federal people had to go along because Alberta became such an important player during the oil boom.

The premier continued this tactic through 1981, when Alberta and Ottawa negotiated an oil-pricing deal in an atmosphere of great national tension and hostility. The federal energy minister, Marc Lalonde, worked out the details with his provincial counterpart, Merv Leitch. Then Lougheed went to Ottawa and struck the final bargain in private meetings with Trudeau. As the country watched, Alberta battled the federal government head-to-head, almost as an equal. Nobody has ever accused Lougheed of having a small ego, but he wasn't merely glorifying himself. His tactic told the nation that the West would no longer be treated as a small-change partner in Confederation. Other premiers followed his lead, although they weren't quite as consistent. Canadians got used to seeing western premiers act as ornery, testy advocates for their provinces.

Partly because of such tactics, the western provinces are excluded from federal-provincial action far less often than they used to be. Western agitation, for instance, helped win all the provinces a strong role in the free trade negotiations. This doesn't change the reality of central power in Canada very much, if at all. But the higher profile for western leaders, as it slowly became part of the national landscape over the past twenty years, at least gave westerners a way of blowing off steam.

Yet this kind of resistance has a fatal flaw; it depends almost entirely on the skills of the premiers who happen to be in power. In the 1970s and early 1980s, the western leaders – especially Blakeney and Lougheed – were remarkably skilful players on the national stage. They also had the advantage of dealing with great issues that united the public in their provinces behind them. Today's western premiers are a punier lot fighting over smaller spoils. At their annual meetings, they are just as likely to squabble among themselves as to unite against Ottawa. In 1989, for instance, when they needed to send a united message on Meech Lake, Getty and British Columbia's Bill Vander Zalm sent signals of weakness by bickering over forestry projects. Ottawa often ignores these premiers even when they do take strong stands; their three-year battle for lower interest rates, for instance, had no effect on the finance minister or the Bank of Canada. This shows that western power, as usual, depends on the ability of the westerners who claim it. The system guarantees nothing.

When Don Mazankowski goes home to Vegreville, the largely Ukrainian community east of Edmonton, he gets very close to the Tories' main modern problem in the West. Beaver River, the riding the Tories lost to the Reform Party in a by-election on March 14, 1989, is right next door. Deborah Grey, a popular high school teacher, won by a huge margin on territory that had been carved partly from Mazankowski's own riding before the 1988 general election. Although many national analysts saw this as a triumph of the western right wing, Grey won with a broad alliance of anti-Tory voters. Frank Sharpe, a New Democrat who lives near St. Paul, a francophone centre, says people from all groups voted for Grey – New Democrats, Tories, Liberals, francophones, Ukrainians. "The provincial Tories could have done something to stop this," he says. "There was really no federal Tory organization because it was a new riding. But the provincials basically sat back and said 'It's Reform time.'" The result was a typical western populist swing, the same kind of damn-Ottawa spirit that has created a string of successful western movements – the Progressives, Social Credit, the CCF, the United Farmers, and, now, the Reform movement. The new party already seems to have the same link with powerful drives and hostilities that rocketed those parties to success. That's why the Tories, from Mazankowski to Prime Minister Mulroney, are so worried about it. They try to brand the party separatist, and warn that a vote for the Reform is a vote for the NDP, but they succeed only in showing how frightened they are.

Once in Ottawa, Deborah Grey surprised many people by refusing to be buried. (She sits as an Independent because the Reform Party doesn't have the twelve seats a party needs to be recognized.) She is friendly, direct and an excellent natural speaker. Ottawa-based reporters who were ready to dismiss her as an unlettered western rube now admit, with some surprise, that they like her. With Grey in Parliament, the Reform Party could no longer be so easily dismissed as just another western splinter group.

A further boost came on October 16, 1989, when Reform Party candidate Stanley Waters won Alberta's Senate election by a landslide, more than doubling the vote of the Tory candidate, Bert Brown. Waters, a former lieutenant-general who commanded all of Canada's land forces, is a true right-winger. During the campaign, standing straight as a broomstick, his face red with emotion, he attacked Canada's stand against the South African regime. He assailled federal spending with similar ferocity. One of his favourite lines was: "I'd like to carve two words into the heart of every politician – cut spending!" Waters stood far to the right of most Albertans, but the voters didn't care; their only goal was to give all Tories, federal and provincial, as powerful a punch as possible.

The election had no constitutional standing and gave Waters no legal claim to be a senator. Mulroney simply ignored him for many months. But his victory was tremendously upsetting to the western Tory establishment, both federal and provincial. Getty was in the absurd position of demanding angrily that the prime minister appoint the fellow who had thumped his party. He was like the cartoon figure who bends over and says, "That was fun – kick me again!" The election was humiliating for provincial Tories, many of whom blamed Getty for bad timing. One of his ministers said privately, "It was a good idea, but why the hell didn't he wait until he had a poll showing we could win?" Worse, the Reform Party victory caused bad feelings between federal and provincial Tories. The federal people thought Getty was trying to embarrass the federal caucus, and the provincials believed Mulroney was rubbing their noses in the defeat by delaying the appointment. Reform Party leader Preston Manning enjoyed this bizarre show, which seemed to prove his main point that a national party can't effectively represent western interests, because it must always fall back on its power base in Ontario and Quebec. Politically, Waters was actually more useful to the Reform Party as a senator denied than he would have been in the red chamber. As Manning said with a laugh, "It doesn't hurt us at all to have him wandering around in sackcloth and ashes, scratching at the door of the Senate." Getty's blundering had allowed the Conservatives' most threatening western adversary to score a tremendous coup. By the time Waters was finally named to the Senate in June 1990, in a side deal to the constitutional bargain that ultimately collapsed, the damage was done.

Partly because of this, by early 1990 the Reform Party was the only political group in the West with any real momentum. It was organizing in British Columbia, hoping to win a by-election in Vancouver Quadra, the riding of former Liberal leader John Turner. In Alberta, the party considered whether to run in a provincial election, and struck a committee to study the question. This group, which included prominent former Tories, was known jokingly as the Task Force to Scare the Hell Out of Don Getty. Manning announced the move at a 7:00 A.M. breakfast attended by 350 of his closest friends. Premier Getty, slumping in public esteem, probably couldn't have drawn so many people at that hour without handing out government contracts at the door.

As its price for staying on the sidelines, the Reform Party demanded that the Conservatives dump Getty and balance the provincial budget. The clear message was: "Reform yourself or we'll kick you out and do the job ourselves." The amazing thing is that the provincial Tories listened. They had no choice, since many of their own MLAS agreed with nearly everything the Reform Party said. Manning, probably the shrewdest politician in the West today, has an impish habit of mailing party literature and resolutions to Tory MLAS. Many of them read the material and wonder if they're in the right party. Manning said, "If you ask whether the creation of this task force is designed to exert pressure on the provincial Conservative party for constructive change, the frank answer is yes." This wasn't as generous as it sounded. By posing as the unofficial reform wing of the provincial Tories, the Reform Party actually sowed discord among them. The party's subsequent decision to stay out of provincial politics didn't remove the threat. It could still decide to plunge in.

Manning is a strange sort of politician. He has the bookish air of a professor, or perhaps a preacher. He doesn't look much like his father, Ernest Manning, the former senator who was Social Credit premier of Alberta from 1943 to 1968, and a lay minister besides. Ernest Manning won seven elections in a row, often by opposing Ottawa from the right. He resisted public ownership of utilities in the province and Alberta still has private utility companies today. He fought against the Liberals' national medicare plan in the 1960s, but the province was eventually forced to join. Preston Manning has all his father's instincts of frugality and mistrust of the state. He also inherited much of his political skill, thoughtfulness and belief in careful strategic planning. As his friends say, he has the political gene. If the federal Tories didn't realize at first that Preston Manning is more than a trifling opponent, they know it now.

Manning didn't spend much time hanging around the legislature as a child, and politics were rarely discussed at home, but he was a careful observer. Sometimes, he concedes, people in the government "would show me a paper that explained how a decision was made. I guess I was always more interested in government than politics. My dad was too, even though he was pretty good at the political end." Years of watching his father fight futile battles for western rights, always without changing the national system, convinced him that something was missing. What the West needed, he concluded, was a regional party that would force

Ottawa to listen – a party like the Progressives in the 1920s, or the Socreds and CCF of later years. Nothing educates a federal government like facing a party that holds the balance of power in a minority Parliament, Manning believes. The powerful influence of the NDP in the minority Trudeau government, from 1972 to 1974, is the best modern example. Manning hopes to be in the same position after the next federal election. His price for keeping the government of the day in office, he says, will be nothing less than constitutional change. He will start with a demand for quick action on western demands for a Triple E Senate (the E's stand for equal, elected and effective). This might happen with amazing speed, Manning feels, if a federal government has to make a choice between acting and losing a confidence vote in Parliament.

"In his last few years in government," Manning says, "my father had come to the conclusion that to advance Alberta's view within Confederation there had to be changes in the federal system. You couldn't do what you wanted just from Edmonton, even if you had 90 per cent of the seats and went to all the federal-provincial conferences." This is why he seems uninterested in being premier, even though many people urge him to run and believe he could win. Instead, he spends his time stumping the West, travelling from Vancouver Island to Winnipeg and back. He flew to Ottawa after Waters's victory to "scratch at the door" for the TV cameras. In March 1990, he ventured into Ontario and Atlantic Canada, looking for converts to his message. The trip to Ontario was well timed; it coincided with rising anti-French feeling expressed by dozens of municipalities that declared themselves unilingual. The Reform Party gets a surprising amount of mail from Ontarians who are just as upset as westerners about federal spending and what they see as favouritism to Quebec.

But Manning's focus is clearly the West. He says: "For the

West to improve its position and change things in a way that could help both us and Canada as a whole, I really think the West has to operate on all fronts. We really do need provincial governments with a strategic grasp of how to deal with Ottawa and how to change it. But I think we also need this sort of initiative in the federal political arena.... We've had strong provincial governments that have tried to bang away, but we'd have no ally in the federal political arena. That's something I think I can do, and there's an opportunity to do it. I'm sort of loath to jump to another tack now."

The Reform Party taps the fury that many westerners feel toward MPS who worry more about pleasing the prime minister than they do about their constituents. The power of this party discipline was obvious in the western debate over the sales tax. By early 1990, only two Tory MPS, both from Alberta, had broken ranks and criticized their government – and were kicked out of caucus for their pains. (The Alberta debate was especially intense because the province has never had a sales tax except for a brief period in 1936.) Manning caught this mistrust of party discipline perfectly during his strong campaign against Joe Clark in Yellowhead riding in the 1988 election. He always drew loud cheers when he said, "Joe's a good MP, but not from here." Manning thrives on the belief that a western politician who goes to Ottawa always sells his soul to the devil, the only question being how long it takes.

Without sounding pushy or self-important, Manning has a canny way of getting his point across. His gentle manner dulls the threatening edge of his tough ideas. And he is shrewdly trying to shuck the party's right-wing image by drawing in members from the centre and even the left. A party is like a hockey team, he says: it needs right-wingers, centres and left-wingers. He wants social activists who will hear arguments about too much spending, and balance-sheet watchers who are sensitive to social issues. "We don't always have to agree, but we have to listen to each other and find solutions," he says. As for the true extremists in the party – the remnants of Western Canada Concept (wcc) and infiltrators from the Western Independence Party – Manning invites people to join and kick them out. "If they say something you don't like, come up to the microphone and tell them what you think," he tells prospective members. "People like that always attach themselves to a new party in the West." If the extremists feel they've lost control, he feels, they will quickly leave and form another splinter group.

All this reveals a sharp western politician who knows how to stand in the middle and let the troops rally around him for a charge at the main enemy, Ottawa. Sadly, charges that the party is anti-French and anti-Quebec don't hurt him a bit (although he denies them). Westerners are in an anti-French, anti-Quebec mood, and Manning expresses the feeling more clearly than any other politician.

At a party meeting in late 1989, Manning turned the tables on Quebec, which set five conditions for signing the Constitution, by making three demands of his own. "If Canada is to continue as one undivided house," he said in a speech, "the government . . . must ask the people of Quebec to commit to three foundational principles of Confederation.... That the demands and aspirations of all regions are entitled to equal status in constitutional and political negotiation. That freedom of expression is fully accepted as the basis of any language policy. That every citizen is entitled to equality of treatment by governments, without regard to race, language or culture."

The party then passed a resolution that virtually invited Quebec to separate if it refuses to meet these demands. The resolution said: "Should these principles of Confederation be rejected, Quebec and the rest of Canada should consider whether there exists a better political arrangement which will enrich our friendship, respect our common defence requirement, and ensure a free interchange of commerce and people by mutual consent and mutual agreement." René Lévesque couldn't have said it better; the Reform Party was really advocating a kind of sovereignty association with Quebec.

Manning expressed the whole spirit of the meeting when he said: "I don't think anybody has called their bluff. We think it's time somebody stood up and said, 'No, we want to put some demands on you.' " And he added just a whiff of western separatism: "We do not want to live, nor do we want our children to live, in a house divided against itself, particularly one divided along racial and linguistic lines."

Manning doesn't worry about being branded anti-Quebec. Ultimately, he suggests, Ontario will prove to be far tougher on Quebec than the West will be. "In Ontario the conventional wisdom in the *Globe and Mail*, at Queen's Park, is that they're all tolerant and receptive to the, 'two languages, two cultures' model," he argued in an interview. "But if Quebec really starts to get serious about secession and Ontario starts figuring out what that will do to its economic interests, I would suspect you'll see a complete change of tone. Some of the most vehement demands that the federal government put Quebec in its place are going to come from those same people....

"In that hour, the West's indifference, in a way, to Quebec, will end up being a blessing. It will be the West that will call for moderation, and say, 'Look, this isn't worth coming to blows over, the way some other countries have when this starts to happen.'" Manning pushes his theory about Ontario's reaction almost beyond credibility, but he is certainly right about western indifference.

Is there a tinge of separatism in the Reform movement, a remnant of Western Canada Concept and other independence groups of the early 1980s? A visit to any Reform Party meeting suggests a strong connection. Many former WCC people, including Jack Ramsay, the ex-RCMP officer who once led the quasi-separatist party, are active in the Reform Party.

Lawyer Bob Matheson, one of the candidates for the party's Senate nomination, used to be involved with the peculiar Confederation of Regions party, which argues that Canada doesn't really exist because the Confederation pact wasn't legal. The Reform Party is also littered with extreme right-wing holdovers from the Social Credit. Partly because of these connections, the party still attracts mainly older people. Early in 1990, an internal party survey leaked to the *Edmonton Journal* showed that, despite its growth, 72 per cent of the members were men, 48 per cent were over sixty years old, and 38 per cent were retired. Sixty-three per cent wanted to stop spending money on bilingualism. Most startling of all, 94 per cent of the members were ready to scrap the Meech Lake accord, even if this caused the separation of Quebec from Canada. The Reform Party expresses useful ideas on national reform, but it also harbours some of the West's most ardent anti-French activists.

The Montreal *Gazette*, in an editorial, noted some peculiar similarities between the Reformers and Quebec nationalists: "The Reformers, for example, think French should be the working language in Quebec and English in the rest of the country; they dislike bilingualism policies. So do Quebec nationalists. The Reformers dislike multiculturalism. So do many Quebec nationalists. Small minds resemble each other the world over."

This is an intriguing comparison, but it doesn't stretch very far. Western nationalists almost always come at Ottawa from the right, Quebecers from the left or the centre. There is little collective spirit in this right-wing western nationalism. It often looks outward to the United States rather than inward to a common western culture (a shaky concept in any case). Western nationalism voices a wide range of solutions, from the Reform Party's slogan THE WEST WANTS IN (a plea for renewed federalism), to Western Canada Concept's bluntly separatist slogan of the early 1980s FREE THE WEST! But the wellsprings are always the same: the feeling that the Prairie West was settled as an inferior, colonial region, and still struggles for an equal place in Canada; the knowledge that the country was frankly built for the economic benefit of Ontario, and that Ontario and Ottawa still see it that way; and the fact that the West is now expected to observe bilingualism, even though it was deliberately settled by the federal government as a multicultural region with English as the common language.

For the foreseeable future, the Reform Party looks like the main carrier of this persistent western virus of alienation. (The strain is certainly persistent; the word "reform" was used as a party name at the turn of the century by Sir Frederick Haultain, the leader of the Northwest Territories.) Through success the Reform Party has absorbed many of the separatists who were thick on the ground in the early 1980s – a dubious and dangerous benefit. But the Reform movement has channelled western alienation into one of its periodic spasms of optimism, toward a hope that the country can somehow be fixed. How long this will last is anybody's guess, but the trend is certainly more appealing than the distilled ugliness of western separatism as it was expressed by Western Canada Concept, West-Fed, the Rupert's Land Independence League, the Unionest Party, the Confederation of Regions, and half a dozen other serious, half-serious, and wing-nut outfits of the early 1980s.

In those days, with rage running high at Trudeau's National Energy Program (NEP), separatism was actually a serious option for many westerners. Some truly astounding things happened. On November 20, 1980, WCC leader Doug Christie, who couldn't draw flies to his movement in his native Victoria, suddenly found himself shouting to a giant crowd of 2,700 in Edmonton's Jubilee Auditorium. Many of the people who thronged to the meeting were not just respectable but the very cream of Alberta Tory society: there were accountants, lawyers, doctors, civil servants, business people and some well-placed individuals very close to Peter Lougheed's government. Some tried to claim they were just observing, but they were caught cheering with everyone else when Christie shouted "Free the West!" Nick Taylor, the provincial Liberal leader who foolishly – or courageously – accepted an invitation to debate Christie, was nearly hooted out of the building. Taylor was a defender of parts of the NEP (to this day he maintains that the companies that complained the loudest about it got the richest from it). This was a dangerous stand on a night when merely to be Liberal was to be in deep trouble. A few Liberals and New Democrats, who had come to keep tabs on the separatists, skulked at the back of the hall, trying their best to be invisible. But Taylor showed a rare kind of courage. He actually lectured the people for being greedy and allowing themselves to be manipulated by the Lougheed government.

"It was a little fearsome," recalls Taylor, who has since lost his party leadership to Laurence Decore. "It was the only time I've ever felt some concern for my safety. People were rushing down the aisles toward the stage. One guy tried to spit at me." After it was over, Taylor says, Christie offered him a bodyguard to see him to his car, but he refused and walked out with his head up.

Christie, who now defends accused war criminals and people charged with spreading anti-Semitic hatred, tried to paint the event as the dawn of a new country. "I have a feeling that this is a moment in history tonight," he told the crowd. "This is not a lament for Canada . . . but a celebration of the birth of a nation struggling to be free." That was about the only positive moment in a rally that bristled with hatred. Christie got the most applause, not for his vision of a new West but for his charge that Trudeau had ducked fighting in the Second World War. Intolerance and racial bigotry were powerful sub-themes of the movement. At another meeting, a man who defended Third World immigration was interrupted by people shouting "Paki" and "Yuki Paki." Nick Taylor says: "They all think the devil speaks French and God speaks English. That's because the Gideon bibles they see are all in English."

Although Taylor and others believed Premier Lougheed was using this feeling for his own ends, the premier was actually in a tight spot. No separatist himself, he was nonetheless forced to show some sympathy for the movement to prevent it from running away with the province. Shrewdly, he never condemned the separatists, realizing that many of them were temporarily furious members of his own party. A good many had the peculiar fantasy that he would suddenly jump up and lead the province out of Canada. His standard line was that he sympathized with their feelings but didn't necessarily agree with their methods. He was playing for time, hoping to cool this sentiment by cutting a favourable oil-pricing deal with Ottawa. To keep his credibility in Alberta, he twice cut oil production and warned Albertans they should prepare to "suffer and bleed." He knew that to a certain point the separatists strengthened his hand in Ottawa. But he also realized that if the movement slipped out of control, it could destroy his government.

The separatist action was centred on Alberta, but it spilled over to Saskatchewan and British Columbia. In Weyburn, Saskatchewan, West-Fed staged the biggest rally ever held in the little city, drawing between 900 and 1,400 people one night in January 1981. Some months later, a pro-federalist group in Yorkton decided to counter all this separatism with a rally in defence of Canadian unity. Nine people showed up. The whole region, even Manitoba, seemed to show growing support for separatism. A poll conducted in early 1981 by the Canada West Foundation, a respected think-tank based in Calgary, found that 61 per cent of all westerners believed that "Western Canada has sufficient resources and industry to survive on its own." Thirty-six per cent wanted the West to go ahead and try. A Gallup poll in the same period showed that 25 per cent of all Prairie westerners, and 20 per cent of British Columbians, expected the breakup of Canada.

There were separatists in western legislatures too. Early in 1980, two Saskatchewan MLAS crossed the floor to sit for the new Unionest Party, which advocated separation from Canada and union with the United States. The leader was Dick Collver, a former leader of the Saskatchewan provincial Tories. They soon found, however, that there was no support for the plan and gave it up. (Collver later formed his own union with the United States by moving to Phoenix, where he still lives. He was a key witness in the murder trial of former Saskatchewan Tory minister Colin Thatcher, testifying that Thatcher rarely called his wife anything but "the bitch.") Few separatists were thinking about what might happen if the West actually left the country, and fewer still were attracted to the idea of joining the United States. Their main impulse was to vent their anger at Ottawa.

On February 17, 1982, with interest rates skyrocketing and oil prices falling, WCC candidate Gordon Kesler won a by-election in Alberta's Olds-Didsbury riding. Kesler, an oil company scout who spent his working days spying through binoculars on competitors' wells, was hailed as the champion of "cowboy power." But his party soon began to choke on its modest success and its own poisons. A convention in Red Deer turned into a fiasco, with factions battling over charges that funds had been misused. Kesler seemed unsure of his own views on separatism; one day he sounded like a nation-buster, the next like a frustrated Tory. He lost in the general election of November 2, 1982, and his party went into decline across the region. By that time the separatist frenzy was fading, as people worried less about politics and more about losing their homes to high mortgage rates.

Western separatism, it seems, is almost always a by-product of good times, when people are feeling feisty and secure enough to indulge their passions. Nothing sends them back to the real world as quickly as a recession. Feeling unequal, westerners often shift from open defiance to quiet surliness and back again. To the psychologist, this might look like a regional inferiority complex; to the historian or anthropologist, it's behaviour typical of colonial societies the world over.

Today, the Yukon and Northwest Territories are in the same subordinate role as the Prairies were before 1905. Pat Michael, clerk of the Yukon legislature, says his territory's status almost exactly parallels that of Alberta and Saskatchewan between 1898 and 1905 – the Yukon has a fair measure of self-government, but no ownership of natural resources, no promise that it will ever come, and no guarantee of provincial status when the Yukon is ready. The familiar colonial relationship has been built into all dealings between the two territories and Ottawa.

Since 1979, Ottawa has allowed the federally appointed commissioner to fade out of decision making and act as a kind of lieutenant-governor. Elected MLAS are now making many decisions. But 60 per cent of the budget still comes from Ottawa and no resources can be developed without federal approval. This leaves tremendous power in the hands of the Department of Indian Affairs and Northern Development, which looms so ominously in territorial life that its clumsy acronym, DIAND, is part of the local vocabulary. Circumstances vary slightly in the Northwest Territories, but the same trends are at work – a bit more self-government but no more real power. The greatest breakthrough on resource control, the Northern Accords of 1988, leads only to sharing jurisdiction and revenue with Ottawa, never to local ownership, even if a final agreement is some day negotiated. No federal government has ever viewed the Yukon and N.W.T. as true equals within Confederation, and the Mulroney Tories are no different.

In one important way, the Territories are in a more difficult spot than the Prairies were when they fought for provincial status and resource control. The Prairies dealt only with Ottawa when they waged these struggles, but the Yukon and N.W.T. must contend with the provinces too. This is a relatively new problem. During the 1979 election campaign, Joe Clark still had enough confidence in Ottawa's authority to promise the Territories provincial status within five years. Everything changed in 1982, when the Constitution was brought home from Great Britain and the provinces won an effective veto over constitutional amendments. Under that formula, no changes could proceed without approval of seven provinces with 50 per cent of the population. Suddenly, in any push for provincehood, the Yukon and N.W.T. were forced to deal with provincial fears and rivalries, as well as with the usual federal morass.

This seemed depressing enough to territorial leaders, but the Meech Lake accord of 1987 was even more discouraging. It proposed a veto over constitutional amendments for every province, a provision that would make northern provincehood unlikely under almost any conditions. Quebec would oppose the creation of two more English-speaking provinces, and Ontario might be frightened by the thought of six potential foes in the West and North. Tony Penniket, the Yukon government leader, describes the problem colourfully. "When the Prairies came in it was like a young kid trying to get the keys to the family car from the parent," he says. "For the Territories, it's like a girl trying to get into an all-male club. You face a blackball from any member, and you don't necessarily know who it might be." The final failure of

Meech Lake robbed the two territories of a constitutional conference on province-hood. "Just when we got a seat at the table, they took the table away," said Penniket.

More surprising, perhaps, the Yukon and N.W.T. get very little encouragement from western leaders. "One of the most disheartening things is the tendency of the western provinces to forget their own history," Penniket says. "While some of them have historically been supportive of our inclusion in such things as first ministers' conferences, we have not been able to count on one of them to defend our territorial interests when it comes to things like Meech Lake. Moreover, at least a couple of times in our history, B.C. has contemplated annexing the Yukon." Penniket's lament is oddly familiar; he sounds just like a western premier complaining about Ottawa.

Penniket also suspects that western premiers aren't eager to see Native premiers around the first ministers' table as equals. He delicately refuses to call this racism; instead, he maintains, it's a fear of having to deal with the Native style of making decisions, which is based more on consensus than on confrontation. Penniket says: "They seem to be thinking, Who are these guys? Where do they come from? How do we deal with them?" Rascist or not, the western premiers don't care to add two more players to the already complicated mix of federal-provincial relations.

For all these reasons, the Yukon and N.W.T. seem doomed to fight the Prairie battle a century or more later, with less chance of success. The struggle might be closer than most Canadians believe. As the West develops, and environmental concern grows, more people will be lured farther north. Once in Whitehorse or Yellowknife, they're often captured for life. As the poet Robert Service said in "The Cremation of Sam McGee": "He was always cold but the lure of gold seemed to hold him like a spell." The Yukon snared NDP leader Audrey McLaughlin from Ontario in 1979, and many more might follow before the century is out. Alaska's population is exploding because it is the last American frontier. As the same feeling builds in Canada, the two territories are likely to become a similar beacon for Canada. But as Penniket says: "There's no plan for the North, no vision about whether it goes somewhere or becomes a Canadian Siberia." As usual, Ottawa has no thought of implanting true political equality on all Canadian territory. Worse, official Ottawa lacks even the awareness that this is wrong and undemocratic.

If there is a true villain in the story of western alienation, it is British colonialism. The founders of Canada, themselves colonials and often proud of it, applied the model they knew when they opened Canada's gigantic share of the continent. It was a terrible mistake. In dealing with the Prairie West, they showed the same failings the British displayed time and again in their rule of the whole empire: strong central control; refusal to consult the local population except under extreme pressure; and a disastrous failure to plan for the future. To the British, the empire was forever: to their students, Canada's Fathers of Confederation, the Canadian West was expected to play indefinitely its role as supplier to manufacturers and seaports, and buyer of finished goods.

Any change from that rigid role, every single one, was won by westerners through agitation, hard-nosed political fighting, and even, in the case of Riel, outright rebellion. In each problem area – the tariff system, freight rates, grain prices, political autonomy, provincehood, resource control – westerners kept pushing until Ottawa finally bent. They used all sorts of devices, from rallies to boycotts and the creation of their own western parties. Peter Lougheed's oil production cuts in 1981 were in the same spirit as the Riel Rebellions. Both were ways of crying out, "No, don't do this to us, listen to us, hear what we say – WE'RE EQUAL!" And all this came about because our Fathers of Confederation were a collection of colonial bureaucrats and merchants, with little vision of a real country and no notion of how to build a federation of equal citizens.

Federal countermeasures to the inevitable resistance have often been fierce and stupid. J.F. Conway notes that between 1867 and 1946, when the federal cabinet often used its power to disallow provincial bills, 122 provincial statutes were overturned. Eighty-six of these, or 77 per cent, were laws passed by the western provinces. In the 1930s the Alberta government went into legal rebellion, passing one law after another to remove the province from the national monetary system. Nearly every one was disallowed, and the sole legacy of those days is the Alberta Treasury Branches, the only provincial depositor's bank in the country. It exists because of an ingenious legal device, invented by Socred premier William Aberhart, that even the Supreme Court couldn't deny; depositors make a contract not with an institution or the government but with a person, the superintendent of the Treasury Branches. This makes the agreement an inviolate personal contract, rather than a deposit under the federal Bank Act. Even today the branches aren't subject to federal regulation, although they have voluntarily joined the Canada Payments Association, which arranges trading of cheques and other instruments for final clearing at the Bank of Canada. "The notion of setting up a personal contract to operate a whole bank had never been thought of before, and it hasn't been done anywhere in the world since," says former Treasury Branches chairman Al Braden. "It was brilliant." Opening an account at the Treasury Branches is an ordeal because so many forms must be signed to make the personal contract airtight, but thousands of Albertans gladly subject themselves to this inconvenience to gain a bit of independence from Ottawa and the chartered banks. The Treasury Branches return the favour a hundred times over. Alberta has the most vibrant rural communities in the West because the branches, unlike the chartered banks, always stay around when times are hard.

If westerners seem pugnacious, stubborn, unreasonably angry, always eager to scrap, total s.o.b.'s sometimes, it's because they have often been forced to battle with Ottawa over such vital matters. The fighting habit dies hard, even in the interludes when a federal government tries to be friendly (as Don Mazankowski and his Tory friends know very well). Unequal at the creation, westerners are like colonials everywhere; they have to be quick on their feet just to stay within sight of the leaders.

The Americans were much wiser, difficult as the notion is to bear, and their history carries an important lesson for Canada. The development of the U.S. Northwest in the eighteenth and nineteenth centuries was relatively free of regional animosity for a simple reason: every new state was created as a legal and constitutional equal to all the old ones. This rejection of the colonial model for internal expansion was quite intentional. Fresh from their War of Independence against Britain, the Americans were eager to purge every trace of colonial poison from their own national system.

As early as 1780, the Continental Congress passed a resolution proposing that new lands "shall be disposed of for the common benefit of the United States, and be settled and formed into distinct republican States, which shall become members of the Federal Union, and have the same rights of sovereignty, freedom and independence as the other States."

On July 13, 1878, the new country passed the Northwest Ordinance, which has been called "the most momentous act in the Confederation's history." It allowed for creation of up to five states out of the Northwest Territory. When there were 5,000 male inhabitants, the Territory could elect a legislature, with the status of a subordinate assembly to Congress, and send a non-voting delegate to the national capital. After any part of the Territory had 60,000 people it could be admitted to the Union "on an equal footing with the original States in all respects whatever."

Historians Samuel Eliot Morison and Henry Steele Commager noted the wisdom and generosity of this gesture:

> The time-honored doctrine that colonies existed for the benefit of the mother country and were politically subordinate and socially inferior was definitely repudiated. In its stead was established the principle that colonies were but extensions of the nation, and entitled, not as a privilege but as a right, to equality. The ordinance of 1878 is one of the great creative contributions of America, for it showed how to get rid of that friction which had always been a canker in the relations of colony to metropolis.

There was plenty of conflict in American westward expansion – between whites and Indians, slaveholders and abolitionists, farmers and ranchers, bandits and the law. These tensions were rawer and more violent than anything on the Canadian frontier, largely because there was no agency like the North West Mounted Police to enforce law and order. There was also a fair measure of regional feeling against those effete easterners, a sentiment still close to the surface in states such as Montana, Idaho and Wyoming. Americans in those regions often resent the economic power of giants like New York and California. Western governors, when they get together for their annual conference, can sound almost as fierce about Washington as their Canadian counterparts do when they attack Ottawa. The western premier who happens to attend (the Americans invite one nearly every year) invariably feels right at home.

But there's a difference – a vast one. An American who lives in Idaho or Utah feels equal, in a political sense, to anyone living in New York or Texas. His or her state has exactly the same rights and powers as every other, including two votes in the United States Senate. An American might whine about taxes, despise the federal deficit, loathe the president, even complain about federal neglect of local economic problems. Some analysts argue that U.S. checks and balances slow down the system, but the citizens rarely feel legally and politically inferior, in relation to federal authority, as a result of living in one state rather than another. The Americans have achieved this despite the shame of slavery and a brutal Civil War that lasted five years. They planted the same spirit even in Louisiana which, like the Canadian Prairies, was purchased (from Spain, in 1800, for $12 million). They did it by promising the inhabitants full rights as citizens and admission to the Union as equals. Compared to this, Canada's treatment of its new territories was miserly and, yes, colonial.

Sadly, the same attitudes live on in modern Ottawa. A subtle colonialism, a feeling that westerners need to be told what's best for them, infuses the capital. This feeling is absorbed even by westerners working in the bureaucracy. They quickly learn that if they want to get ahead, they must drop the rhetoric of grievance and the western tendency to butt impatiently at problems. The road to advancement is paved by the national system, not by regional history.

Westerners return this condescension with images of their own. To them, one of the most powerful Canadian stereotypes is of the lazy, wasteful, slow-moving, dim-witted Ottawa bureaucrat. Some of these people seem to wake up only at lunch hour, when they hit the bicycle paths and jogging trails provided by the national taxpayer. In the cafeterias scattered around Parliament Hill and in the public buildings downtown, they ate cheap subsidized food for years, until they were finally forced to pay something closer to world prices. The same people start the suspiciously early traffic jam in the capital every Friday at about 2:00 P.M. Far worse are the corrupt, crooked MPs and senators who drag the whole country into the muck. All these types have coloured the West's view of Ottawa, but they aren't the whole story.

For every one of these people, there's a civil servant who works hard, takes the job and the country seriously, cares deeply about the government's duty and image, never condescends to anyone. For each MP or senator who gets by on bluster and bribes, there are many others who work fifteen hours a day, visit their ridings every weekend, help their constituents out of every imaginable scrape and wouldn't take a bribe or a kickback if the alternative were slow death. These are the true public servants, the moral holdovers from the days when Canada had one of the best, most devoted bureaucracies in the world, and a Parliament Canadians could respect.

They are people like Dr. Sheila Wynn, an Albertan, who worked killing hours to advance women's rights before she left Ottawa to be an assistant deputy minister of the environment in the British Columbia government; Ottawa-born Peter Fleming, the director general of radio for the Canadian Radio Television Commission, who scours the country to make sure the broadcast rules are obeyed, and leaves only friends behind; Arthur Kroeger, deputy minister of employment and immigration, who has been a strong, steady advocate of western interests over his long career. Among politicians, there is Mazankowski, who seems to run half the government without attracting a whiff of political trouble or scandal; Speaker John Fraser, who rose from the bizarre tuna scandal to become one of the best modern Speakers, the man who single-handedly saved the Commons from choking on its own bile; NDP leader Audrey McLaughlin, a warm woman who vaulted amazingly from obscurity to national fame, but still hangs out the laundry in summer at her little house on Hoge Street in Whitehorse; Windsor West Liberal Herb Gray, a political Clydesdale whose tenacity inspires admiration, even though he's no particular friend of western interests (he still laughs about the "four-second sitting ovation" he got in Edmonton during the oil crisis). These people are in it because they care about Canada.

And yet, with the best will in the world, they are all in some degree afflicted by the most pernicious Ottawa malady of all – system blindness – a tendency to believe that the problems are tough, but the basic structure of the country is sound. These people are so busy patching the cracks that they never examine the foundation. Any new government that takes office quickly loses any interest it had in structural reform. (Constitutional tinkering is always so political, and so focused on Quebec that it merely brushes past the real problems.) Drunk with the headiest intoxicant of all, public trust, the politicians believe they can solve every problem themselves with goodwill and hard work. The Tories after their 1984 victory were the classic example. With the biggest majority in Canadian history, including 58 of the 77 western seats then available, they truly believed the western millennium was at hand. They showed little interest in Senate reform or other structural changes. Mazankowski, Jake Epp, Bill McKnight, and the rest of the western Tory elite seemed to feel that their mere presence in cabinet would end discrimination against their region.

Many people believed this myth of western power. In Ontario and Quebec, a new stereotype of government by the all-powerful western cabal emerged, causing a good deal of suspicion and resentment. A long article in *Saturday Night* magazine described how westerners were running the country. Even westerners, who should have known better, believed a new era was beginning. Mazankowski recalls: "Conservatives in Western Canada essentially thought that the Conservative party was their political movement. The expectations were fairly high. There was a sense that in very short order all the ills that affected Western Canada would be rectified. Of course that's difficult to do because all policies have to be tailored within the context of the national public interest. Within that context, I think we have leaned over backwards in dealing with some of the chronic irritants that affect Western Canada."

Mazankowski argues that major structural problems have been solved with the introduction of free trade, the elimination of many tariffs and the ending of discriminatory freight rates. But this is only tinkering on a slightly deeper level than usual. Canada remains a badly built federation, the only one in the western world with no effective forum for settling regional disputes, with no alternative to crippling party discipline, without escape from the majority rule of most populous regions. We are a decrepit, nineteenth-century colonial federation, where the very idea of an elected Upper Chamber was a joke only a few years ago.

Until the country is repaired, until the engine itself is completely overhauled, westerners will feel angry, Quebecers embittered, and Atlantic Canadians ignored. Bob Edwards was partly right. We have first-rate problems that can never be solved with a fourth-rate system. Westerners have sensed this for generations, but Ottawa, blind to its own bad genes, tinkers the nation away. This is our great national tragedy, for so much needs to be done, and still could be done, if the times were right and our leaders had the will.

TWO

My Light Wasn't There

WESTERN CANADA IS GROWING UP. WESTERN CITIES are thriving and maturing, western population is rising, westerners are reaching for achievements that seemed hardly possible a decade ago. From Victoria to Winnipeg, the region pulses with creative energy and activity – in the arts, in business, even in politics. More westerners are accomplishing things to be proud of, to emulate, to hold up as beacons of western pride. Instead of leaving at the first sign of economic trouble, many are staying home to make their careers against whatever odds. Of many examples, one of the best is Anne Wheeler, the Edmonton-based maker of such movies as *Loyalties*, *Cowboys Don't Cry*, and *Bye Bye Blues*. Wheeler's working life is a daily affirmation of the fact that with vision and will, anything can be done in the West. But it isn't easy, and her latest film, *Angel Square*, proves the point very well.

It's March 1990, and *Angel Square* is having a devil of a time. The children's film about mitt-to-mitt combat on a winter playground was supposed to be shot in Hull or Montreal. A lack of suitable locations drove it out of the Ottawa area, then conflicts with the Quebec government agency that funds movies chased it away from Central Canada entirely. Now the movie is back in Wheeler's home town, Edmonton, rewritten for the second time, and waiting for snow. This is a Christmas movie, but Edmonton looks barren, as brown as sourdough. At 7:00 A.M. on the day shooting is to start, crews are hunting desperately between buildings and down back alleys for mounds of grimy late-winter snow, then trucking it to the central location, an area flanked by three red brick buildings – a school, a library and the old Edmonton bus barns. Every day the children in the film plot elaborate ethnic attacks and snowball fights. But today the location doesn't look much like a winter scene, despite the best efforts of the snow-scroungers. *Angel Square* needs a miracle.

Amazingly, it comes on cue. At 7:30 A.M., as the technical crew arrives to prepare for the first day of shooting, a few flakes flutter down. How nice, Wheeler thinks, a little flurry will look good in the schoolyard shots. She doesn't dare hope for a real storm. But by 8:00 A.M. the snow is falling hard, and by nine it's a blizzard, the second heaviest of the year. The crew members cheer and throw snowballs. The children in the movie – dozens of young actors and extras gathered from Quebec to British Columbia – have a fine time pelting each other for the cameras. Six inches of snow pile up over the day, and *Angel Square* is saved. "It must have been the prayers," jokes one crew member. "Everybody was praying. I'm not religious, but it sort of makes you wonder."

The greater miracle is Wheeler's survival as a western-based maker of major feature films (the budget for *Angel Square* is over $3 million). She has been wooed by Toronto and Hollywood, and virtually invited to take these offers by jealous people in her own film community. Only a week before *Angel Square* began shooting, her previous film, *Bye Bye Blues*, was passed over when the Alberta Motion Picture Industry Association handed out its annual awards. The prize for best production went to a one-hour made-for-TV film called *Life After Hockey*, rather than to Wheeler's full-length epic based on the life of her musician mother. *Life After Hockey* is an amusing and original little movie, made by Wheeler's friend, the talented Tom Radford, but the two films belong on separate rinks. Shot in India and Alberta, *Bye Bye Blues* played for long runs in western cities, and was nominated for thirteen national Genie Awards, including best picture, and won three. Denys Arcand's *Jesus of Montreal* won, perhaps deservedly, but Wheeler's fine film certainly merited a better fate in her own province. The stakes may be smaller in Western Canada, but the rivalries and jealousies are big league.

Garth Hendren, Wheeler's husband and business partner, sometimes marvels at her tenacity. "The energy you must devote to these battles – as well as raising money and other things – reduces productivity, and you can burn out sooner," he says. "It's an exceptional person who stays."

Yet Wheeler has good reasons for remaining in the West. Alberta has become a lively centre for film-making; in fact, Glynis Whiting's film *Bloodclan*, a $1-million thriller starring Gorden Pinsent, was shooting in Edmonton at the same time as *Angel Square*. "That's not happening anywhere else in the country," Wheeler says. "There's still an enthusiasm here for making films that's very rare in Canada. I have the same group around me that I've had for three films. There's a style we're developing that eventually, we feel confident, will make its way out to the big world. We've also been nurturing an investment community and an audience. You need those things to make movies.... Toronto and Vancouver, the bigger centres that would normally draw someone like myself, are making far fewer indigenous movies." Only Quebec film-making has more vitality, she says, although Manitoba's film industry is growing with the works of people like Greg Klymkiw, and Merit Jensen.

Wheeler has another, simpler reason for remaining in Western Canada. She loves the place and the people with a quiet, lyrical passion. Sometimes she seems almost haunted by rural westerners and their striving against economic depression, isolation and limited opportunity. (*Bye Bye Blues* and *Cowboys Don't Cry* both relied on such themes.) She identifies passionately with western warm-heartedness and sense of community. But the powerful Toronto-based film critics seem to think her people are corny, almost too good to be true. She was surprised and wounded when Jay Scott of the *Globe and Mail* ridiculed *Bye Bye Blues* (and badly hurt its chances for success in Ontario). His review began: "*Bye Bye Blues*, Hello Kleenex," and went downhill from there.

"But my characters are very true to life," Wheeler protests. "There are lots of people like this in the West. I always remember a woman who was an extra in *Bye Bye Blues*. She was in it for about two seconds, but she met a lot of the crew. We came back to her town about six months later, and she came walking onto the set with two shopping bags. She said, 'Hi sweetheart, I brought you some Christmas baking because I know you have children and you probably don't have time to do it this year.' So she gave me two whole bags of baking, everything you can imagine."

Another part of the same film was shot in Old Glenora, Edmonton's ritziest neighbourhood, but the people didn't seem any different. "I had brain surgeons out there stopping traffic for us," Wheeler recalls. "The whole neighbourhood – doctors, lawyers, accountants – they were out pushing cars and helping us lug equipment." Although the scenes didn't make it into *Bye Bye Blues*, Wheeler's people got the same treatment when they came back to Old Glenora to film parts of *Angel Square*. The crew was flooded with coffee, trifle and cookies. "Trifle," one crew member muttered in amazement, "they gave us trifle."

The western countryside obsesses Wheeler as much as do the people, and she is almost fanatical about scouting for locations that reveal the West at its most magnificent. "It always amazes me to see a tiny shack out in the middle of a field with one tree beside it," Wheeler says. "You know someone lived in that house and planted that tree and probably had kids, and weathered the winters, and endured all that, and their grandson is probably an accountant in Edmonton or Toronto. The people who came out here in the early part of the century were remarkable. I cast my locations as much as my actors. I try to use the landscape as a character, one that initiates the drama rather than reacts to it." This sense of landscape as actor, as a cause of events and an influence on lives, is probably stronger in the West than anywhere else in Canada. People like Jay Scott don't seem to realize that Wheeler isn't just shooting pretty landscapes; she is explaining why westerners feel and act the way they do.

Wheeler has driven down nearly every back road in Alberta to search for stark, dramatic locations. A stunning scene in *Bye Bye Blues* shows the results. Rebecca Jenkins, who plays Wheeler's young mother, walks along the edge of an Alberta coulee above the Red Deer River. The camera sees her from far-off, as she proceeds slowly across a ridge, a tiny figure in a landscape that rolls endlessly into the infinite western sky. The scene explains at once why her character is so tough and independent. Such images are breathtaking on film and even more mesmerizing in real life.

The brilliance of the light and the way it caresses the vast western landscape captivate Wheeler. She was almost glad when *Angel Square* was forced to abandon Montreal, she says, because she couldn't visualize the scenes in the sluggish light of Central Canada. "My light wasn't there," she says. "I didn't have my shadows, I didn't have my sun going at a certain angle across the sky. Now that I'm back here shooting, things just look right.... In most places, the sun just goes down, but here, in summer, it lingers for an hour and a half on the edge of the sky. You can afford to do a whole scene in this wonderful golden bath of light. It's very special."

Westerners in general see these things, feel their power, take strength from their message of freedom and limitless space. From Winnipeg to Victoria, through the prairies and the mountains down to the coastal rain forest, such stunning sights and images abound. They are no more beautiful than the Gaspé, the Ontario lakes or the Maritime shores, but they are unmistakably western, somehow bigger and freer than other Canadian landscapes.

West of Kenora, even the sky seems to broaden and deepen in anticipation of the beckoning plains beyond. The light grows richer and clearer, igniting the familiar – brick buildings, red boxcars, fields of ripening wheat and yellow canola blossoms – into slashes of molten colour. Robert McInnis, one of the best landscape painters in the West and perhaps all of Canada, says he feels liberated every time he approaches the prairies. "Many times I've driven across the country," he says, "and coming out of the lake areas of northwestern Ontario toward Winnipeg I always breathe a sigh of relief. I'm no longer closed in by the massive green. I suddenly encounter the feeling of openness and vastness. There's a sense of power out there. You don't feel this in Ontario, you don't feel it in New Brunswick. All these things do something for us inside and affect our emotions."

Prairie westerners don't always recognize their powerful attachment to light and open space, but they sense it soon enough when they go to the East. McInnis, who grew up in Saint John, now finds Central Canada and the Maritimes "oppressive and claustrophobic." McInnis recently spent three years in Ottawa and found that his painting suffered. The apocryphal Saskatchewan farmer said it best in a joke: "Mountains are nice, hills are fine, but they spoil the view." The feeling isn't limited to artists and farmers; Lloyd Axworthy, the Winnipeg Liberal MP, once remarked that he feels liberated whenever his plane lands at Winnipeg airport. Ontarians and Quebecers are sometimes bored or even threatened by the prairie vastness; westerners often feel suffocated by the more constricted landscapes of Central Canada.

When the prairie light hits the Rockies, westerners are transfixed. The luckiest man in Alberta might be Ian Tyson, who left Toronto for a ranch near Longview with an inspiring view of the mountains. Tyson raises cutting horses and runs his vigorous singing career from a spot regularly described by visitors as the most beautiful place in the world. The 'sixties folkie who wrote "Four Strong Winds" and other standards is now a proud crooner of pure cowboy songs. "Toronto may be rhythm and blues," he wails, "but if you migrate here, you'll be howlin' at that old Alberta moon." Few singers in Canada, even the Quebecers, display as proud a sense of place in their music. Even in his first hit, "Four Strong Winds," Tyson thought he'd "go out to Alberta, weather's good there in the fall." In one recent ballad, the narrator awakes "to find that Calgary girl watching the morning light." Singing joyously about the end of the disastrous Alberta-Saskatchewan drought of 1988, Tyson evokes a strange and haunting image: "It's like Africa tonight across that plain, since the rain." Few places in Canada seem much like Africa, but the southern prairie on a dry summer night has an uncanny likeness to the plains of Kenya or Tanzania. Gaze into the cottonwoods by a riverbank and you almost expect to hear a lion cough. Tyson was raised in British Columbia, learned his craft largely in Toronto, is heavily influenced by cowboy tales from the United States, and rides his cutting horses in American competitions. But there's no doubt where this foothills boy belongs. He's a westerner, and in the West he means to stay, even though the chances for fame and riches might be greater elsewhere. There are thousands like him.

This is a new phenomenon. For many years, westerners with artistic ambition went to Toronto or the United States as a matter of course. Others, average people who simply needed to make a living in bad times, flocked to Ontario. The smallest upward blip in the Ontario economy drew westerners like a magnet. Peter Lougheed, the former Alberta premier, called this "sending jobs down the pipeline to Ontario." For generations, western politicians were preoccupied with finding ways to keep the native sons and daughters at home.

But a remarkable thing happened in the middle and late 1980s. While Ontario's economy exploded with the hottest growth in a half-century, the population of three western provinces continued rising. Only Saskatchewan lost people, and the depletion wasn't very serious – a net loss of only 4,400 from January 1, 1985, to January 1, 1990. (Many people in Saskatchewan, prompted by rhetoric from Opposition politicians, believe that in 1989 the population dipped below one million for the first time since 1984. But Statistics Canada figures show that the total was 1,001,600 at the beginning of 1990.) Westerners still went to Ontario, but they often stayed for short periods rather than settling down. Some who left were replaced by other migrants, including people from Ontario itself. Ontario was no longer a vortex that sucked in huge numbers of westerners; just as often, it repelled them.

Ontario's population grew tremendously between 1985 and 1990. It jumped from 8,969,200 to 9,667,600, an increase of 698,400, This certainly cut into the rise of western population. But in the same period, B.C.'s population went over three million for the first time, climbing from 2,863,000 to 3,105,700, a gain of 242,700. Alberta, too, did much better than most people believe. During the oil price crash of 1986 and 1987, the province actually gained a few thousand people. From 1985 to 1990, the population rose by 109,700, from 2,339,200 people to 2,448,900. Manitoba's increase was more modest but still steady. The population grew from 1,060,600 to 1,086,600, for an increase of 26,000.

Today, many westerners resist moving to Southern Ontario because they can't afford housing or don't like the size and frantic pace of the Toronto area. Western business people who once saw a transfer to Toronto as the ticket to success now face a tough choice between career and family. Quite often they refuse the offer because the social and economic costs of a move are simply too high. Visiting westerners return with horror stories about nightmarish traffic, sky-high prices, increasing crime, and a growing contrast between wealth and poverty. Toronto is gaining a reputation in the West as Canada's New York; it has wonderful amenities, but the hassle of finding and enjoying them is too exhausting. Westerners return to their cities – Winnipeg, Saskatoon, Victoria – with a new appreciation of their beauty and relaxed pace. And these cities, as they grow quickly in maturity and sophistication, offer many of the same comforts and diversions with few of the problems. A good cup of Italian coffee is as easy to find in Calgary or Regina as in Toronto. All the major cities have their theatres, symphonies, art galleries and other cultural resources. Four western cities – Winnipeg, Calgary, Vancouver and Edmonton – have NHL hockey teams, all better than Toronto's. The best-kept secrets in Canada are Calgary's Kensington area and Edmonton's Whyte Avenue, with their funky shops and restaurants. Torontonians and Montrealers who land in these neighbourhoods are often amazed to discover that anything so original and diverting can exist west of their cities.

Many Torontonians and other Southern Ontarians are at last discovering the quality of life in western cities. They're also recognizing the financial benefits of moving west; since mid-1989, at least, western realtors have been finding homes for Torontonians who see the sense in selling a house for $500,000 and buying a bigger and better one, with lower taxes, for $200,000. When Toronto buyers come west, they're the ones who pay more than a house is worth because western prices seem ridiculously low. Realtors get big eyes whenever they see a Torontonian coming. From Winnipeg to Victoria, the happiest phrase in the business these days is, "I've got a Toronto buyer."

In a smaller way, there are signs of a similar exodus from Vancouver. Some people, weary of heavy traffic and high prices, are filtering across the water to Victoria, or back over the mountains to Alberta. In ten years, says one recent reverse migrant, Vancouver will be "a long thin Toronto," subject to similar pressures and problems. "Vancouver used to be a big city that was easygoing," says Edmonton-based film-maker Dave Cunningham. "Now it's just big. Fifteen years ago, we'd go there to get away from the pace in Edmonton. Today it's the other way around." Like nearly everyone on the Prairies, Cunningham always welcomes a business trip to Vancouver, but these days he's also glad to return.

For the first time ever, there's a feeling in Alberta and B.C. that real estate is desirable because outsiders covet it, not because of a temporary resource boom. Hong Kong money is a powerful factor in this surge of western development. The initial burst of investment from the Crown colony went to Toronto and Vancouver, but by early 1990 it was pouring into Alberta as well. Oriental buyers avidly snap up apartment buildings and houses. An Edmonton widow sold her family home in Edmonton for more than $600,000, only to see it knocked down to make way for an even more lavish residence. A man who was renovating his house was approached by a recent immigrant from Hong Kong who said: "I've got five houses. Can you do those too?" Things have changed greatly since 1983, when Hong Kong investors told Lougheed that Alberta was too cold to interest them. Economic heat has made them reconsider, and the temperature was turned up quickly after the massacre of students on Tiananmen Square on June 4, 1989. Hong Kong residents who hoped for democracy in mainland China lost their illusions and began looking in earnest for new homes in western North America. When this activity began to cool because of higher interest rates, westerners were predictably angry at the Bank of Canada.

For all these reasons, it's easier for westerners to remain in their region than it used to be. With the possible exception of Saskatchewan, where farm problems have been devastating, there's a new feeling that for years to come much of the national action will be in the West. Westerners are no longer so likely to dream of living somewhere else; more and more, they feel that the places they once yearned for are becoming untenable and their own are getting better. The frontier spirit still lingers in a uniquely western ethic of friendliness, co-operation, hard work and volunteerism. At the same time, the cities are increasingly sophisticated and complex. This is a precious combination that might be difficult to hold in proper balance (indeed, it could already be collapsing in Vancouver). But many westerners are determined to enjoy it while it lasts.

"If you're so good, why are you still here?" Holger Petersen has heard and sensed the question dozens of times in his career as a western musician, radio host and record company executive. His Edmonton company, Stony Plain Recording

Company Ltd., produces records for Tyson, Amos Garrett, the Downchild Blues Band, Spirit of the West, and for several American musicians, including John Prine. Stony Plain is Canada's most successful label for roots and country music, with a distribution network in Japan, West Germany, France, the United States and several other countries. Petersen hosts a national show on CBC radio, "Saturday Night Blues," and a province-wide show on CKUA, the Alberta educational radio network. The Alberta program has endured for twenty years to become the longest-running blues show anywhere in Canada. Stony Plain recordings have won four Juno Awards. Not a bad list for a westerner who drifted into the music business twenty years ago. But still the doubting question comes, Why does he stay in the West?

This is the perfect western question, distilling all the inferiority and doubt, all the lack of confidence in judging talent by western standards. It's a regional version of the same question "national" figures hear when their reputation spreads across the country: if you're so good, why are you still in Canada? But a Holger Petersen doesn't have as much trouble explaining his choice as he once did, either to himself or to the outside world. "I like the size of Edmonton," he says. "You can be more productive. There's less travel time involved in everything you do, and not as much opportunity for shmoozing. Living in a community outside the mainstream gives you a different perspective on the major centres." He has a distributor and publicist in Toronto and the industry people there are very supportive, he says. But any urge to live in Toronto always passes in a hurry.

In Petersen's business, the assumption that everyone should work in the national metropolis is unique to Canada. He points out that, in the States, the hottest music scenes are spread all over the map – not just in New York and Los Angeles, but also in places like Indianapolis, New Orleans,

Cincinnati, Memphis, Chicago, San Francisco and even Austin, Texas, or Akron, Ohio. Americans don't see why the artists and facilities should squeeze into one or two major centres. Talented Canadians will begin to stay in their own places, Petersen argues, "as more and more people in the business in Toronto want to get out and begin looking for alternatives. It's expensive to live in Toronto, and the place isn't as soulful as it used to be."

John Gray, the musician, satirist, brilliant writer of musicals, and inventor of wild music videos for CBC's "The Journal," finds an uneasy regional peace in Vancouver. Born in Ottawa and raised in Halifax and Truro, Gray ended up on the West Coast because his wife, Beverlee, lived there, and he was "the variable." A devout nationalist and member of the Council of Canadians, he strives to write and perform for all Canada from one of its extremities. "If I can't write for the whole country, I'd rather not do it at all," he says. "I'd rather change countries entirely." There's plenty about the West Gray doesn't like – the focus on money, puritanism that stifles expression, the lack of culture among entrepreneurs. "They don't read novels," he says. "Working people do. Farmers in Saskatchewan are better read and more thoughtful." In the West, says Gray, "the arts are not money-friendly.... To express things is self-indulgent."

Yet Gray has made Vancouver his base for a remarkable career as a writer of musicals. Billy Bishop went not only to war, but all across Canada and eventually to Broadway. *Rock and Roll* was a solid hit, *Health* twisted the musical into new shapes, and *Don Messer's Jubilee*, inspired by a popular old TV show, raised deep questions about national identity. Most of Gray's work has been well received everywhere but in Vancouver. "It's that old attitude you find so often – if you're so good, what are you doing here?" This is part of the colonial attitude that Gray says he expects but doesn't resent. In fact, he likes the sense of artistic isolation he sometimes feels in Vancouver.

"You don't get that clubby feeling you get back East," he says. "I don't benefit as a writer by running with a crowd. I find myself imitating others. It's not that healthy." Gray was even more blunt in a 1989 interview with Southam News. "There's nothing so debilitating as being in a room with a lot of people you don't really like," he said. "That happens in Ontario more than anywhere else. It happens because there's a kind of facile nationalism, which is really what I call 'Ontarioism,' which is really an Upper Canadianism and therefore hard to take sometimes." Like many Canadian nationalists who live in the West, he feels that Ontario's parochial nationalism, which so often assumes that Ontario speaks for the nation, is the worst enemy of the national unity. If Gray weren't in Vancouver, he says, he'd prefer to live in Quebec.

Saskatchewan artist Joe Fafard knows exactly where he belongs – in Regina, where he has lived for many years. Born and raised in the francophone community of Ste. Marthe, Fafard is best known for his imposing, original sculptures of cows and other farm animals, which are snapped up eagerly by collectors everywhere in Canada. Seven of his remarkable cows are on startling display near the Toronto-Dominion Centre, a quirky rural reminder in the most urbanized spot in all Canada. Fafard has never regretted his decision to stay in the West. Years ago he established his own foundry to strike his bronzes because there was nobody else to do the work. Today it employs six people. Had he lived in Toronto or another big city, he says, he would have made a deal with somebody else's shop. "I'm better off in the long run," says Fafard, "because I'm in control of the results. It helps my art to control the process from beginning to end. There's no problem working out of Regina as a visual artist. You can move art anywhere."

When people ask in condescending amazement why a man so talented would live so far from Southern Ontario, he asks seriously why they live so far from Regina. "There's more activity in art in Toronto," Fafard says, "but that doesn't seem to make it better art. There's no advantage to my work in living in Toronto. Saskatchewan's a good place to live as an artist." When he visits, he finds Toronto "hardly livable." There is more choice, but not enough time to enjoy it.

Fafard embodies a special brand of western pride unique to Saskatchewan. The province isn't as self-satisfied as B.C., as angry and blustery as Alberta, or as touchy and explosive as Manitoba. Saskatchewan has the smallest population and the weakest economy of the four western provinces, but the people seem to know themselves, feel their identity, more completely than any other westerners. Lorne Nystrom, the NDP member of Parliament from Yorkton-Melville for twenty-three years, says the province tends not to be as angry because it hasn't so often been singled out by Ottawa. The National Energy Program of 1980 was mainly an Alberta outrage, and the CF-18 decision was a humiliating defeat for Manitoba. When the federal Tories tackled the provinces in the 1990 budget, they cut the rate of funding increase to British Columbia and Alberta and cancelled major projects in both provinces – the Polar 8 icebreaker on the west coast and the OSLO oil sands development in northern Alberta. Saskatchewan, being poorer, usually avoids such direct assaults. Things might not be given, but they are rarely taken away.

Yet Ottawa has never really been a friend, so Saskatchewan residents are forced to rely on each other to overcome their disadvantages. They created medicare and the NDP (although the party's predecessor, the CCF, was formed in Calgary in 1932). Roy Romanow, the provincial NDP leader, argues that Saskatchewan has more collective spirit than any other province. Politicians get in trouble when they try to run against this feeling, he says. This is why the Saskatchewan Tories took such a beating in the polls in 1989 when they tried to privatize Crown corporations.

Fafard expresses this co-operative feeling as well as anyone: "We don't think the world revolves around us, and since it doesn't, we tend to make things happen if we want them to." This leads to a relatively low level of alienation in a province that has cause to feel more. Fafard, in fact, doesn't feel alienated as a westerner at all, but he is angry about his treatment as a francophone. "The most difficult problem living in the West is being a French Canadian here," he explains, "and being denied the opportunity for education in French."

Fred Keating brings an American eye to the West. An immensely talented actor, TV producer, writer and public speaker, Keating was born in Columbus, Ohio, and raised in Detroit. He has worked in Los Angeles and once had a play produced off-Broadway in New York. In his youth he often crossed the border to sample the pleasures of Windsor, he says, but "I never came to Canada until I came West." Eternally busy at everything from hosting TV awards shows to performing on radio, he now bounces around a circuit from Edmonton to Calgary and Vancouver – "the West's golden triangle," he calls it.

"I think I feel more Canadian because I come from somewhere else," Keating says. "I've had the quintessential Canadian experience, giving up family and friends to come here." He loves Western Canada because he often gets the feeling he's working in a new industry and doing things for the first time. "In most established cities, like Toronto and New York, the ladders of success are obvious. I could predict where I'd be five years or ten years down the line just by looking at other people in that neighbourhood. Here I don't know those things, and it's great. The opportunities are as endless as the horizon."

Keating especially admires the willingness to work hard that he finds on the Prairies. He could probably make more money in Vancouver, but he chooses to live in Edmonton with his wife and young family because of the work ethic and the quality of life. "I feel like I've landed in paradise compared to growing up in the west end of Detroit," he says. "The things I measure success by aren't location or income. They're the kind of work you have and the way you live. I've got all I want right here." Toronto, admirable as it is, doesn't attract him because "the weather is awful and the environment is terrible. I'm not willing to trade my life and my lungs to live there."

Mel Hurtig has probably bucked longer odds than anyone else to remain in the West. He not only established Hurtig Publishers, the first company to produce national-market English books outside Ontario, but threw himself into eternal warfare with the prevailing political forces in Alberta. Once a Liberal, always a fierce critic of western Tory policies like free trade, a founder of the Council of Canadians, Hurtig has been threatened and insulted in his beloved home town, Edmonton. Hurtig is always saying things western Conservatives don't want to hear: he warns about the dangers of foreign investment; derides the Free Trade pact as the "Americanization of Canada Agreement"; cites the dangers of selling off oil and gas to the United States; and details the flow of profits to American companies. During the Trudeau years, his nationalist stand made him one of the most unpopular men in Alberta. He not only held his political ground, but produced one of the most impressive feats in Canadian publishing history – the three-volume *Canadian Encyclope-*

dia. Hurtig risked even that when he came out publicly against free trade. Alberta government funding was crucial to the first encyclopedia, and the Tories were not pleased with his statements. In both his political and business life, Hurtig would probably be more comfortable in Toronto.

He decided early on to stay in the province where he was born. Partly it was stubborn pride. Hurtig recalls how Torontonians laughed when he talked about setting up a publishing house in Edmonton. "They all said the same thing," he says. "It couldn't be done anywhere but Toronto. All the editors, designers, buyers and press were there." But Hurtig began his little company in a ramshackle building beside a busy overpass. Hurtig Publishers has gone on to produce eight number-one best sellers, two editions of *The Canadian Encyclopedia*, and the new five-volume *Junior Encyclopedia of Canada*. Even Hurtig's political enemies are forced to respect his courage and iron will. Today he has the deep satisfaction of seeing the province swing slightly toward his views. All but two Edmonton MLAS are New Democrats, and doubts about free trade are growing. Hurtig reports that people now approach him in restaurants to congratulate him on his stand.

To Hurtig, a westerner isn't defined by the way he or she thinks. He notes, correctly, that westerners follow doctrines that cover the whole political spectrum. "I get sick and tired of journalists from Central Canada painting Western Canada as if it's one entity," he says. "There are profound differences within the region and even within each province. For instance, there's an enormous political and cultural gap between southern Alberta and north and central Alberta. And the politics of a Don Getty have little to do with the politics of Manitoba or Saskatchewan." Also, westerners are routinely painted as right-wing rednecks in the Ontario media; yet Hurtig, and thousands of westerners like him, have been fighting these people all their lives.

"I never wanted to leave Western Canada. I enjoy the quality of life here," he says. "Edmonton has all the amenities – good theatre, the University of Alberta, restaurants, a multicultural society. I love the climate, even in winter. Every day I take my dogs for an hour walk in the river valley. People are really very friendly, open and warm. There's a sense of being able to do almost everything if you try hard enough." Mel Hurtig himself is the proof.

From Winnipeg, businessman Izzy Asper sees the West very clearly – it's as a colony of Central Canada, he says. As head of CanWest Television Group, which won control of Global Television in late 1989, Asper wants to create programs that show westerners as they really are, not as stick figures in melodramas of crop failure and drought. Westerners are fed up with seeing themselves in hokey images cooked up in Central Canada, he says.

Asper led the Manitoba Liberal party from 1970 to 1975 and was an early agitator for Senate reform. He is absolutely fierce on one point – he insists the country isn't built right. In fact, Asper ran one of his election campaigns on a platform of refederating the country. The nation will never work properly until all the provinces are treated equally at one level of government, he insists. More and more westerners agree with him, and because of this, Senate reform is becoming a powerful western demand. The Meech Lake accord ran into western resistance because it seemed to block the road to structural change. This opposition showed that westerners, contrary to most opinion, don't necessarily want stronger provinces; they want a stronger Canada with an equal voice for themselves at the centre.

Most of the people portrayed in this chapter, even those who aren't political, express some form of this conviction. They feel that even when they achieve their goals in the West, they do so in spite of powerful forces that control the country. Some, like Hurtig, don't feel very troubled by this. "I've always felt I could beat the bastards whenever I had to," he laughs. Others, like Asper, are deeply angry about unequal treatment. Above all, westerners hate to have their lives and work considered second-rate because they aren't living in the places others define as important. To them, the West is no hinterland. It's the centre of their proud universe, a rich and gloriously beautiful region that lacks only one thing – political equality.

THREE

They Love You When You're Gone

IF HIS MANNER AND FERVENT PROTESTATIONS ARE any guide, Brian Mulroney yearns to be loved in the West. You can see it in his hopeful, longing smile whenever he gets off a plane or mounts a western podium. Like any eager suitor, the prime minister comes with gifts and favours – a Western Diversification Initiative here, a jackhammer for the National Energy Program there. Often he seems to govern through a tacit alliance of Quebec and the West that virtually ignores Ontario (the classic example was the 1988 free trade election campaign). In 1986 he gave Saskatchewan premier Grant Devine $1 billion after a single phone call. The suitor brings loving words, too. His first view of the scenery around Grande Prairie, Alberta, he recalls, was of the most magnificent thing he'd ever seen. "This was the splendour of Western Canada unfolding for me."

Alas, the West does not swoon. After a tentative embrace

in 1984 and 1985, most westerners now think of Mulroney as the blind date they're sorry they accepted. Mulroney has three major problems in the West. First, his personal style and rhetoric are profoundly at odds with western expectations of a prime minister. Second, his words have led westerners to expect basic changes Mulroney has not delivered, and perhaps never intended to. Third and most important, he is no more able than any other prime minister to overcome the basic unfairness of the country. Ultimately, all Canadian leaders fall back to the populous fortress of Central Canada if they intend to survive. And Brian Mulroney certainly means to survive.

The Mulroney style, an odd blend of private charm and public smarm, carries the precise scientific formula for setting western teeth on edge. "He always seems to be very self-satisfied," says Gurston Dacks, a respected political scientist at the University of Alberta in Edmonton. "You think he expects a choir of angels to break out singing whenever he speaks. This is contrary to the western style, which requires people to be more self-effacing. They place some value on humility, and they don't find it in Mulroney." A senior bureaucrat of a western government puts it more bluntly: "He uses big words, fancy words, almost as if he's speaking some kind of ancient courtly English. And you get the feeling you can't believe a damn thing he says." The same feeling is magnified in the rural West, where Mulroney comes across as a slick big-city lawyer despite his own small-town roots.

Michel Gratton, Mulroney's press secretary from June 1984 to March 1987, and now a Toronto *Sun* columnist, targets the prime minister's image problem in the West. "One of the things that bother westerners is that he campaigned [in 1984] as the son of a truck driver from Baie Comeau. But as time evolved, and as all the stories started to come out about his lush travels, his expensive clothes, the image emerged that he'd forgotten his roots. The phoniness in Mulroney is now hurting him more in the West than anywhere else." Mulroney appeared in casual sweaters in the West when he ran for the Tory leadership in 1983; now he always looks as if a valet just draped the latest elegant jacket over his shoulders. Casual westerners have a sharp eye for such inconsistencies.

In private, with just a few people, Mulroney can give a very different impression. He exudes sincerity, confidence, and genuine concern for Canada and the West. His speech is softer, less elaborate, as if the absence of TV lights somehow extinguishes the blarney. His whole manner inspires confidence and invites friendship. This helps explain why Mulroney kept the loyalty of his entire cabinet, and most of his caucus, when the Tories dropped to 15 per cent in the polls in early 1990. A politician with no virtues doesn't manage a feat like that. But Mulroney's considerable private skills do not translate into public appeal.

Part of this problem is built-in, because Mulroney's identity is closely linked in western minds with his background as a Quebec politician. Westerners regard Quebec politics as inherently more venal than the western variety, despite ample evidence of lusty trough-snorting in their own region. So they have long memories for the prison that suddenly moved to Mulroney's home riding, for criminal charges against some of his MPs and ministers, for the space agency that landed conveniently in Montreal, for the huge increase in regional development money that went to Quebec after the 1984 election. More even than Pierre Trudeau, Mulroney seems to pop right out of a free-wheeling Quebec tradition of blatant payoffs. Western Tories are constantly forced to battle this impression that, because of Mulroney's influence, Quebec will always win.

"Damn it, he's the whole problem," says an Alberta official. "He governs only for Quebec. He's done a lot for the party, I'll grant you that. But I just can't bring myself to like the guy. He's such a bullshitter."

Image is a massive problem for Mulroney in the West, but it's merely the symptom of more substantial failures. David Kilgour, the MP for Edmonton-Southeast who was booted out of the Tory caucus in April 1990, has constantly warned Mulroney that he must change not just rhetoric and image, but the whole focus of national government. Even before the forced divorce from his party, Kilgour called for an end to federal purchasing habits that always favour Ontario and Quebec, more research and development funds, a reformed Senate, true respect for the "regions," more freedom for western Tory MPs to speak their minds and vote with their consciences.

In Kilgour's view, Mulroney talks a good western game and offers a few cosmetic changes to dupe the public, but still governs for Quebec, his own province. "I am part of the anti-Mulroney thing," Kilgour said in an interview. "Mr. Trudeau was perceived to be a prime minister for Ontario and Quebec. Mr. Mulroney is perceived to be a prime minister only for Quebec. What we need is a man or woman who will be a prime minister for all Canada.

"I've been driven increasingly to this view," Kilgour added bitterly. "To be honest, my skin crawls whenever I talk about this government in the West. In my view, Mulroney is going to do the same thing, and more, to the Tory party that Trudeau did to the Liberal party. He's become far more a part of the problem than the solution. He's a creature of contempt and ridicule."

A large part of the problem is structural, Kilgour feels, and Mulroney has done very little to solve it. "Great gobs of regional development money are going to Toronto. In the West we're running at about 21 per cent of federally funded research and development, when on a population basis we're entitled to 30 per cent. We did a little study in my office, and discovered that of 220 top policy makers in Ottawa, only 10 per cent were born and educated in the West. Atlantic Canada, the West and the North add up to about 15 per cent of the top people. That's a large part of the problem as far as I'm concerned. These people look at a map and we might as well be in Zaire." In his view, Mulroney has missed a golden chance to change these attitudes – perhaps because he shares them.

Kilgour always had a great flaw in the eyes of some Conservatives – he's John Turner's brother-in-law. Many have long regarded him as a traitor for speaking out against Tory policy, especially when the party was low in the polls and his stands were popular in his home riding. But Kilgour won nomination and re-election in 1988 when the party establishment wanted him out. His 1988 book on western alienation, *Uneasy Patriots*, earned praise even from critics for being thoughtful and fair-minded. Kilgour has probably done more research on the substance of western alienation than any other MP. And there's no question that he accurately reflects the anger of many westerners.

Mulroney's personality and Quebec identity boil vigorously in fevered western minds to form a potent political poison. When the prime minister talks about regional equality, westerners hear blarney; when he does a favour for his riding, they think they see the real prime minister. Mulroney knows this all too well. As he told the authors: "I think that because I'm from Quebec, and represent a French-speaking riding, and elected a lot of members from Quebec, and from time to time have taken stands that favour Quebec, that that offends people."

According to Mulroney, westerners forget the number of times he has advanced their interests. "I've overridden all kinds of bureaucrats to come down in favour of important matters involving Western Canada. That tends to be forgotten." Mulroney cites federal support for a heavy oil upgrader at Lloydminister, free trade, the Western Diversification Initiative, and the dismantling after 1984 of the National Energy Program and the Petroleum and Gas Revenue Tax (PGRT).

Many westerners were pleased with these measures, but Mulroney failed to get full credit because of bad timing. In every case but the free trade deal, the prime minister didn't act decisively until western protest prodded him to perform. This was very frustrating to western Conservatives, including former Alberta premier Peter Lougheed. Before the 1988 election, Lougheed urged Mulroney to follow through on his western promises quickly. "There's no point in raising hopes and then delaying action for so long that resentment is even deeper than it was before," Lougheed said in an interview.

Many westerners were furious, for instance, that it took Mulroney a full two years to dismantle the hated NEP. "People felt it would have been done at once for Ontario or Quebec, without any delay at all," says political scientist Gurston Dacks. The recession that struck in 1982 reversed the oil-price spiral that provided Ottawa's only rationale for the NEP in the first place. Yet the federal government continued to take revenue from some parts of the program long after Mulroney's Tories were elected in 1984. To westerners, it seemed that the prime minister was bowing to the revenue-hungry Treasury Department led by Bay Street darling Michael Wilson. As a result, some of the resentment aimed at the Trudeau government was needlessly redirected at Mulroney's own. Today he gets very little political credit for tearing down one of the most discriminatory policies ever aimed at a Canadian region.

This is stranger still in light of Mulroney's genuine abhorrence of the NEP and the thinking behind it. The very thought of the program still makes him angry because it violates all his beliefs about national fairness. Mulroney's fury is so intense in private conversation that he must be either completely sincere or a far better actor than Canadians know.

"The National Energy Program was a uniquely pernicious action, without precedent in the history of Canada," he charges. "I think it was a fundamentally evil thing to have done. And it was wilfully done, too, for reasons that I think were a lot more . . . political than economic."

Of course, many Canadians approved of the NEP, including a good number in the West. To Manitoba and mainland British Columbia, especially, it never seemed to be such an atrocity, because people in those places shared the national impression that Alberta was growing too rich. Yet Mulroney pinpoints several undeniable truths about the NEP. The Liberals used it to stop the westward flow of wealth; they intentionally tried to lure an industry out of the provinces to lands controlled by the federal government; they changed the rules to accomplish this; and they never did such a thing to Ontario or Quebec. The effect – and probably the goal – was to check abruptly the growing influence and financial clout of Alberta, Saskatchewan and B.C.

Mulroney knows all this as well as does any westerner. He might have been a hero for years in Saskatchewan and Alberta if he had acted quickly on his beliefs and struck down the NEP in the first weeks after taking office. But by lingering over the decision for too long, he planted the first damaging impression that, like Trudeau before him, he always places other interests before those of the West. In David Kilgour's opinion, there's one reason for this: "He talks a good game about the West, but he really doesn't give a damn." The polls show that this is a common western belief. In 1989 and early 1990, Environics Research Group found in its regular surveys that westerners were as convinced as they had been in Trudeau's day that Ontario and Quebec run the country. "We're finding the same level of alienation, even though the West supposedly has all these people in power," explains Donna Dasko, Environics vice-president.

The factors playing against Mulroney become almost overwhelming when mixed with that eternal western irritant – language policy. Even though the prime minister surely means well, time and again he makes himself look like a hypocrite who sees only Quebec's side of the language story.

Westerners remember how Mulroney came barrelling into Manitoba in 1983, during a fierce court-inspired debate over French services and translation, to lecture about language rights and disown his own provincial Tory party. Yet he was extremely reluctant to criticize Quebec when that province overturned a Supreme Court ruling against Bill 101 in late 1988. The result of Quebec's action was Bill 178, which forced English indoors, prompted unexpectedly angry reaction in the West and threatened the Meech Lake accord. In language policy, especially, Mulroney always seems to coddle his own province and scold the rest of Canada. This strikes many westerners as supremely unfair, even though most of them are far less interested in French rights in the West than they are in English rights in Quebec.

All these factors combined in early 1990 in a great western fury against the proposed goods and services tax. Especially in Alberta, where there was a sales tax for only one brief period in 1936, the anti-GST coalition cut across every conceivable political divide. It united New Democrats with Reform Party members, Tories with Liberals, western separatists with devoted federalists, union leaders with the business community. No federal initiative since the NEP was more universally loathed, and this one, arguably, was even less popular in British Columbia, Saskatchewan and Manitoba, where the NEP had always enjoyed some support.

Jim Dinning, Alberta's education minister, said the goods and services tax accounted for at least three-quarters of the

Tories' terrible showing in the polls. It was hard to dispute that assessment on October 16, 1989, when Albertans sounded a giant raspberry at the prime minister and his tax by choosing Stan Waters, the Reform Party candidate, as the province's Senate nominee. By this time, veteran Tories such as Ron Nicholls, a former provincial party president and a key organizer for Mulroney in the 1988 federal election, feared that Albertans could easily turn to the Reform Party, at least federally, if the tax were not withdrawn. The tax, a serious enough grievance on its own, had become a symbol for all the anger and disappointment westerners felt about Mulroney. "There's still some respect left for the Conservative party," said Donna Dasko of Environics, "but the feeling about Mulroney is remarkably negative."

The prime minister is certainly out of touch with many westerners, including Conservatives, on the whole issue of Senate reform. He agreed to the principle of major Senate revision in the Meech Lake accord, but when Alberta decided to hold its peculiar election, the prime minister was far from enthusiastic. He insisted that the final right to choose senators was his alone, and noted that the accord required the provinces to submit several names, not just one. He was on solid constitutional turf in saying this, since Alberta in a way was grandstanding outside the Meech Lake agreement. And he was in tune with his own party loyalists who expect a Tory prime minister to give these patronage plums to them, the truly deserving, not to some elected upstart from another party. But Mulroney's anti-election stand was extremely unpopular with many ordinary westerners who felt he was denying their democratic right to choose their representatives.

The truth is that neither Mulroney nor any of his key western ministers, from Deputy Prime Minister Don Mazankowski to External Affairs Minister Joe Clark, really agree with the idea of a Triple E Senate (elected, effective and equal). They feel that western grievances spring from political neglect, not structural problems, and that they are the heroes to right the balance. Of course, they never mention that a truly effective Senate would dilute their own authority and challenge their right to represent the region. On this issue, Mulroney sounds as centralist as any Ontario politician – and so do some of his western ministers.

And yet, despite this remarkable record of blunders and misjudgements, no prime minister since John Diefenbaker has tried harder to win over the region, or been so convinced of its real importance to Confederation. No leader born and raised in Central Canada has had so much sympathy with western aspirations or so much understanding of small-town western life. No prime minister in history has dismantled so many policies prejudicial to the region, or erected so many friendly ones. And Mulroney, alone in recent memory, dared to run an election campaign based on a main platform – free trade – hotly opposed by the Ontario government. Trudeau never had the nerve to buck Ontario, for all his vaunted toughness.

Free trade, no matter what one thinks of its underlying philosophy or ultimate impact, destroys once and for all the National Policy of high tariffs that had favoured Central Canada, and especially Ontario, since Confederation. A majority of westerners always considered it a blatant tool for colonization, a device for holding the West forever as a captive market to Ontario and Quebec. They well remember the spirit, if not the words, of Liberal prime minister Wilfrid Laurier's declaration to the Canadian Manufacturers' Association in Quebec City in 1905:

> They [the western settlers] will require clothes, they will require furniture, they will require implements, they will require shoes – and I hope you can furnish them to them in Quebec – they will require everything that man has to be supplied with. It is your ambition, it is my ambition also,

> that this scientific tariff of ours will make it possible that every shoe that has to be worn in those prairies shall be a Canadian shoe; that every yard of cloth that can be marketed there shall be a yard of cloth produced in Canada; and so on and so on...

The policy worked beautifully – manufacturing tripled between 1890 and 1910. The trouble was that 80 per cent of this growth was in Central Canada. This federal dream for developing a region turned into a nightmare when waves of people poured into the new land. The West was ready to create a sophisticated economy, but tariff policy stood like a wall, permanently blocking the region's development.

As the West evolved in this stunted fashion, and the National Policy made it clear that "Canada" really meant "Central Canada," western hopes hardened into disgust and disillusionment. Alberta felt so alienated and outcast by 1935 that William Aberhart's Socreds tried time and again to remove the province from the national banking system, but the Supreme Court of Canada blocked their quest six times. For more than a century, many westerners regularly made two general demands on Ottawa – abolish the National Policy, and implement free trade with the Americans. Tariff policy was often changed, even softened, to respond to these movements, but no prime minister until Mulroney had the courage to satisfy both grievances at once.

And yet, when Mulroney accomplished these goals after one of the toughest election fights in the nation's history, and defied the Ontario government in order to do it, westerners were strangely unimpressed. They tended to regard even this remarkable political feat as yet another sop to Quebec. After all, Mulroney's home province wanted free trade, too, so that had to be the whole reason for his stand. Hardly any western commentators mentioned the death of the National Policy, and precious few gave Mulroney full credit for free trade. Thus he failed to make major political gains among western supporters of the policy, while earning the lasting hatred of a large number of westerners, chiefly in Saskatchewan and British Columbia, who were bitterly opposed to free trade all along, and remain so today.

Despite all these problems, Mulroney believes that westerners will some day realize he has their best interests at heart. There is a huge difference between him and Trudeau, Mulroney feels, because the Liberal prime minister chose to govern against major western interests, while he always tries to accommodate or at least consider those interests. Judging by both his words and his actions, there is little doubt that he is sincere about the intention, even if the performance is often dismal.

"The West had always been penalized by the National Policy because of its failure to have access to the Central Canadian market," he says. "One of the effects of the philosophy was that the West always lost. You weren't always sure who benefited. Some days it could be Ontario, some days Quebec, some days someone else. But the one certain factor was that no matter how thin you sliced it, the West always lost."

There is more sympathy in these few remarks than Trudeau showed at any point during fifteen years as prime minister, despite his many travels in the region and his surprisingly keen understanding of western history (most westerners assume he knew hardly anything about their past, but this was far from the truth). Mulroney sympathizes with western alienation, perhaps because his roots in small-town Quebec enable him to recognize the symptoms and feel the emotions. Trudeau, the patrician Montrealer, seemed to feel that westerners would rather whine about their history than overcome it. He revealed this feeling during an interview in Winnipeg in August 1980, just after he had won a thumping national majority, but with only two seats in all Western Canada.

"Why do you westerners let five little pip-squeaks from Quebec run the country?" Trudeau suddenly demanded, irked by questions about his failure to comprehend western alienation. "Why don't you take it over and throw us out?" The best way to do this, he suggested, was to vote Liberal and then bend the governing party to the West's will. How this could be done when Ontario and Quebec controlled the vast majority of seats in Parliament, Trudeau did not explain. But his attitude to the West was clear enough: to him the problem in the region wasn't a lack of political power, but a failure of will power.

Mulroney's appreciation of historical injustice toward the West is much deeper. Major changes were needed to place the West at last on an equal footing, he argues. Westerners have never lacked will or courage, only the tools to use it in their own interests.

"When I had to make the decision about free trade," he says, "one of the major things that I thought it would correct would be a historical injustice . . . that had been, I think, unintentionally inflicted upon Western Canada originally. I don't think anybody set out with any malice to devise a straitjacket for Western Canada, but one originated."

Mulroney's central belief about Canada – the vision he is so often accused of lacking – is that the country will be strong if the regions and provinces are strong. He does not believe, as Trudeau did, that the national will is always best expressed by Ottawa or Parliament. It grows naturally out of regions that are confident; sometimes it is voiced by premiers, sometimes by MPs, sometimes by the federal cabinet; but always it depends on the belief that all regions are equal, at least in opportunity.

This comes very close to the "community of communities" notion that proved so disastrous for former prime minister Joe Clark. The phrase implied that every part of the country is equal, and that no one institution, not even

Parliament, has final authority. Clark never really believed this; he is a man of Parliament to his bones. But the country came to believe it, and the impression helped cost him an election in 1980.

Mulroney is much shrewder. He speaks in vaguely romantic terms about Canada being "a country of small towns and big dreams." He conceded in the Meech Lake accord that all provinces are equal, and that provinces can participate in the naming of senators by submitting lists of nominees (but no elections, please). Legally, he has tried to go farther than Clark ever did toward the "community of communities." But politically, he is more careful not to give offence and provoke a centralist reaction. With his standing in the polls, he hardly needs more problems.

Essentially, Mulroney trusts Canadians in all regions to form the national character. He seems genuinely to feel that the views of a British Columbian or Albertan are as valid, as Canadian, as those of any Quebecer or Ontarian (although people in the Yukon and Northwest Territories argue with justice that Mulroney, by refusing to encourage provincehood in the Meech Lake accord, considers them second-class citizens). Purely partisan feelings are another matter. In the heat of debate, Mulroney seems to despise all New Democrats and Liberals equally, no matter where they're from. And he has absolutely no tolerance for anti-French feeling in Western Canada or anywhere else.

Mulroney's sympathy for the West seems to be a natural part of his heritage. As a small-town boy from Quebec, he recognizes familiar values of neighbourhood and community in the rural West. The Quebecer in him has an instinctive empathy for western feelings of alienation from power bases in Toronto and Ottawa. Bob Rae, the Ontario NDP leader, observes that Mulroney always seems extremely uncomfortable in Toronto and doesn't function well there.

"I've always thought that Western Canada's needs were

in harmony with the aspirations of Quebec," the prime minister says. "They both suffered by comparison with Ontario.... It's not that Ontarians are smarter, are better educated or more courageous, it's that they have the benefit of geography and historic government policies.

"I used to say that Canada is a country of small towns and big dreams . . . and it is! It is exactly that! And it's the product . . . all the product of small towns. And the farther you are away from things, the more you tend to articulate and give expression to your own dreams."

The striking thing about these comments is how western they sound, even though they spring from Quebec experience. Westerners often miss this link, this common alienation that they share with Quebecers, because they perceive that Quebec is firmly inside the national system. The great irony, of course, is that most French Quebecers see exactly the opposite; they believe that they are the outsiders, while the vast English-speaking West is part of the power ranged against them. These feelings are so rooted on both sides that even when western and Quebec politicians co-operate on a major issue, as they did in 1988 when they took steps to limit minority language rights in both regions, the significance is missed entirely. Because westerners tend not to see these connections, Mulroney's effusive comments about the West come off as insincere. When he talks about "the splendor of Western Canada unfolding for me," the words seem forced and corny.

The prime minister has tried very hard to cultivate political alliances in the West. Indeed, he has often gone to great lengths – even extreme ones – to help his allies, even though they often forget his favours when the political tide turns against him. The classic example came during the Saskatchewan election campaign in October 1986, when Mulroney rose in the Commons one Friday to announce that the government intended to give western farmers $1 billion in aid. The only premier he mentioned, by curious coincidence, was Saskatchewan's Grant Devine.

The next day, the *Saskatoon Star-Phoenix* printed a fascinating account of the strange events that led to Mulroney's statement. Earl Fowler, a *Star-Phoenix* reporter pounding the campaign trail, was awakened from a deep sleep in his motel room at 5:30 A.M. by the sound of Devine's voice. The reporter almost missed the significance of what was going on, because Devine was speaking so loudly he thought the premier might be in the middle of a telephone interview with a radio station. Fowler nearly rolled over and went back to sleep.

But he stayed awake, and learned that Devine was talking to Tory ministers in Ottawa, pleading for aid. He said grain farmers were in deep trouble because of low prices and needed assistance quickly, preferably before voting day in Saskatchewan, October 20. "If I lose this, it's going to be damned tough on Mulroney the next time around," the premier said, apparently referring to the federal Conservative party's chances in his province. Mulroney took note – within three hours, he was on his feet in Ottawa to announce the payoff.

That was a big favour, and Devine has never quite forgotten it, even in the darkest times. Unlike the other western premiers, he was even mildly sympathetic at first to the federal proposal for the sales tax, arguing that if it had to come, it should at least be as fair as possible. He was tenacious in his support for Meech Lake long after it began to lose favour among the voters in his province. As one wag in the Regina legislature press gallery says: "When Grant gets bought, he stays bought."

But Devine finally drifted away from the prime minister on the tax issue, and even on the delicate question of Meech Lake. In the summer of 1988, he was one of the first premiers to argue for saving the deal through a "parallel accord," a set of negotiated items to be attached to the original deal. This solution didn't appeal at the time to Mulroney or Senator Lowell Murray, his minister for federal-provincial relations, because they then felt, as Murray said with admirable foresight, that "to reopen Meech Lake is to kill it."

Mulroney has done good deeds for other western premiers, too. The dismantling of the NEP, however belated, was a move of great benefit to the three westernmost provinces, and especially to Alberta. It's no coincidence that Peter Lougheed quietly supported Mulroney over Joe Clark at the 1983 Tory leadership convention: he knew that Mulroney might be easier to deal with on this issue.

In 1979, when Clark was prime minister, Lougheed had a great deal of trouble with his fellow Albertan over energy policy. Clark didn't simply fall into line with Alberta's demands, but tried hard to produce a policy that would serve all interest groups. At one joint meeting of federal and provincial Tory caucuses in those days, held at Government House in Edmonton, Lougheed blasted Clark's Alberta Tory MPs (there were no other kind then) for failing to support his view of Alberta's interests. Clark wasn't there, but Don Mazankowski, as loyal in public to Clark as he would later be to Mulroney, was furious. The private meeting signalled a serious rift between the premier and the prime minister. And it showed how a western prime minister is sometimes forced to twist himself into knots to show he isn't favouring his own province.

By contrast, Lougheed always got on well with Mulroney. In 1983, when Ontario premier Bill Davis was considering a run at the federal Tory leadership, Lougheed let it be known that he would do everything he could to turn western Tories against Davis. Lougheed's clear choice was Mulroney, who had made his bitter feelings about the NEP clear very soon after it was released in 1980. When Mulroney took office in 1984, he owed Lougheed a great deal, and he kept his word, even though he took his time doing it.

At first the prime minister also got on very well with Lougheed's successor, Don Getty, who took over in 1985. Getty was reasonably patient about the delays in scrapping the NEP, and he was very enthusiastic about free trade. During the 1988 federal campaign he buried his worries about the sales tax and endorsed free trade in appearances with Mulroney in Alberta.

After the 1988 election, though, Getty suddenly became very troublesome. In March 1989, the premier ran an Alberta election campaign that focused heavily on opposition to the sales tax, and on Getty's plan to hold a Senate election unwanted by Mulroney. This campaign featured far more Ottawa-bashing, in fact, than any conducted by Lougheed during the height of the great western wars with Trudeau. Lougheed's immensely successful tactic was to set up a strong anti-Ottawa climate, and then rarely mention the federal government during his campaign. He knew that if he attacked Ottawa and lost even one seat, the federal government would consider him weaker. Getty never seemed to grasp this basic truth about successful Ottawa-bashing in Alberta, and, remarkably, he was opposing the federal leader of his own party.

Ultimately this hurt the Alberta premier, because many Tories in his province are members of both the federal and the provincial parties, and they resented being asked to choose between leaders. Partly because of this, Getty's Tories lost support in their 1989 election and the premier was even defeated in his own riding of Edmonton-Whitemud. (He later won a by-election in the rural riding of Stettler.) But the episode showed Mulroney's curious inability to hold the loyalty of a western leader who had benefited from his policies.

Mulroney didn't have much more luck with the other western premiers. Within three months of the federal election, Bill Vander Zalm in British Columbia was expressing serious doubts about Meech Lake, and raging at every opportunity against the proposed sales tax. Ottawa should make deep cuts to spending instead of levying a new tax, Vander Zalm said at the annual premiers' conference held in Quebec City in August 1989. As a premier who had balanced his budget and even produced a surplus, he was a very cocky fellow.

It was Manitoba's Gary Filmon, however, who became Mulroney's nemesis in the West. Clinging precariously to power only with the fragile support of Gary Doer's Manitoba New Democrats, Filmon was forced to be extremely sensitive to public opinion on language and the Constitution. At the time, Manitobans were enraged that Quebec had overturned a Supreme Court decision while their own province was still translating laws into French because of a 1983 court order.

In December 1988, Filmon bitterly attacked Mulroney's reluctance to criticize the new Quebec language law. He then used Bill 178 as his excuse to withdraw a legislature resolution to ratify Meech Lake. An all-party committee spent nine months hearing witnesses and then drafting an extremely critical report on the accord, which Filmon defended at the divisive first ministers' conference held in Ottawa from November 8 to 10, 1989, at the Government Conference Centre. This led Mulroney to compare Filmon unfavourably to his NDP predecessor in Manitoba, Howard Pawley.

Filmon set the prime minister off by saying that after a good start in federal-provincial relations, the federal government had started behaving in ways that recalled Pierre Trudeau. The Liberal era, Filmon said, "was marked by an attitude in federal circles that failed to understand or respond to the concerns . . . of people beyond the boundaries of the federal capital.... We see echoes of those memories today." Filmon then fired a dart at Meech Lake by saying: "While the Meech Lake accord was created as a positive effort to cement the unity of our nation, it has since become a symbol of disenchantment and disunity." While voicing these lofty sentiments, Filmon was also writing letters of support to anglophone protesters in Quebec – a tactic that infuriated both federal officials and Quebec bureaucrats.

Mulroney retorted that Manitoba's hard line on Meech Lake threatened to return Canada to a time when there was little understanding of francophones. "For all of us with a passing acquaintance of Canadian history – the rights of English and French minorities over one hundred years – it was a matter of special significance, special pleasure, to see the premier of Manitoba sign the Meech Lake accord in this room three years ago."

Then came what Filmon later called the "cheap shot." Mulroney said: "There was a lot of symbolism, a lot of significance in what [former premier Pawley] did that day... it took a great deal of statesmanship, for which I was particularly grateful." Mulroney spoke quietly, but he looked furious.

"Wow, I guess we must have said something to upset him," joked one Manitoba official, marvelling at Mulroney's casual insult to a fellow Tory during a meeting broadcast on national TV. Many observers felt that the prime minister, increasingly exasperated by provincial bickering, was beginning to sound as testy as Pierre Trudeau had at combative federal-provincial meetings in the bad old days.

Mulroney's treasured western coalition was in tatters by the beginning of 1990. All the premiers were opposed to the sales tax, and Meech Lake had become a live hand grenade that they wanted to toss back into Mulroney's lap. On the streets, from Winnipeg to Vancouver, comments about the prime minister were becoming as aggressive and hostile as anything heard about Trudeau a decade earlier. ("I hate them both," one Albertan said, "but Trudeau was at least an honest man.") In Alberta and British Columbia, the Reform Party was rising ominously, like the spectre of the CCF or the early Social Credit party, becoming a powerful new voice of western protest on the federal scene.

It's hardly surprising that Mulroney doesn't claim to be entirely comfortable in the West, especially in British Columbia. "There is a politicized dimension to public life in British Columbia that I wasn't used to," he says. "The first time I confronted it, it was brand new to me. It's kind of like a constant collision of people, ideas, and a certain amount of . . . brutality is too strong a word, but even for someone used to hard-nosed politics, it's a little unusual."

Michel Gratton gives a more vivid account of Mulroney's private feelings about the West, including British Columbia. "As far as B.C. is concerned," says the former press secretary, "he has the same impression as a lot of easterners, that half the people there are crazy.... The media's just so wacko over there. They'd rather do a piece on the shoes he's wearing than what he says. He'll answer every question for five minutes, and then they'll show him walking away. At first he got along with Vander Zalm, though. He was a very charming kind of guy, but since then his opinion has drastically changed. He seems to think he's a political liability....

"He hates going to Manitoba," Gratton says. "The reason he hates it is because he knows they hate him. He told me that once. He despairs of trying to make the West understand his view of Quebec. That's the sort of thing that makes him very uncomfortable....

"He seems to be fairly comfortable in Saskatchewan, but he hasn't felt comfortable in Alberta since Lougheed left. That's mainly because he doesn't get along with Getty. And he certainly doesn't like the Reform Party. It's alien to everything he believes in. He has left Alberta to his strong ministers, especially Don Mazankowski. It's almost as if

Maz is the prime minister as far as Alberta is concerned.... When he campaigned in the Pembina by-election [in 1986], he went on stage with Lougheed, not Getty." Gratton suggests that Mulroney wanted to punish Getty.

The brief campaign whistle-stop in Pembina riding, near Edmonton, certainly couldn't have impressed Mulroney with Alberta. While giving his pitch for the Tory candidate, he suddenly stopped cold because he thought someone in the audience had called him a "frog." To the surprise of many who hadn't heard the remark, he launched into an angry lecture about tolerance. Some reporters thought Mulroney had invented the insult for his own convenience, but a check later turned up several senior Tories and New Democrats who had heard the remark, and much worse besides. Mulroney was apparently a victim of a group of hard-core Alberta separatists who packed the front of the audience. Given his strong and genuine feelings about French language rights, such episodes can hardly give him a warm feeling about the West.

Whatever the prime minister has given the region, many westerners still fear it might all be taken back some day by a rapacious federal government, or by Mulroney's own in a different mood. In Calgary, the eternal question is: What happens if oil prices go to $50 a barrel? The automatic answer is always the same: Ottawa would find a new way to take a large chunk of the money – in effect, it would recreate the National Energy Program in another form. The habit of feeling oppressed dies hard; it even gets comfortable after a time. Most westerners refuse to admit that Mulroney's relatively benign approach might last through his second term.

Says Ron Ghitter, a former Alberta Tory MLA who is now a prominent businessman and lawyer in Calgary: "I think Ottawa can still snatch it away.... They still have the taxing authority. You think a federal government wouldn't do that? I think they would do it in a second."

Peter Aubry, a francophone oil company executive in Calgary with bitter memories of the NEP, says everything is "the same as ever" between the West and Central Canada. "We send them the raw product and they sell it back to us in a can," he snorts. Aubry recalls that when he worked on the railroad as a student in North Bay, Ontario, his home town, there was a chart on the wall that showed prices for shipping goods around the country. "I always wondered why it cost more to send an item from Calgary to North Bay than the other way around. Exactly the same item. Now that I'm in the West, I know." The system has always been rigged to favour Central Canada, he says.

To these and other charges, Mulroney says that his government is putting unfair treatment "out of reach" for its successors through such devices as free trade. But he acknowledges that Ottawa's taxing authority is undiluted. "Anyone malicious enough . . . with the power to tax, can do anything they want.... Still, I don't think it [the NEP] can be repeated. I wouldn't want to be the guy trying it."

And yet, sadly for the prime minister, westerners feel after six years of his government that not much has changed except a few symbols. Free trade is a nice gesture that brings vague opportunity but few concrete results. Saskatchewan native Ray Hnatyshyn is a good choice for Governor General because his appointment shows that bilingualism isn't always vital to Canada's survival, but a Governor General can hardly change the world. The goods and services tax at least applies to the whole country, not just the West, but it still is a genuine political atrocity. The prime minister got rid of the NEP, yet he could hardly have done anything else, and he was damned slow getting around to it. To every friendly move by Mulroney, there is a handy western response to show that the federal system is as hostile as ever. All the Don

Mazankowskis, Jake Epps, Joe Clarks, Bill McKnights, Kim Campbells, and other westerners, packed into the centre of Mulroney's cabinet and arguing for the region, never seem to dent this bedrock western view of how the country works.

But Mulroney the suitor doesn't give up. He recalls past gestures of affection as proof that the majority of westerners still like him and his policies. "We know that at the end of the day it's kind of all right," he says, "because look at the vote [in 1988]. If Western Canadians. . . had felt there was anything fundamentally unfair, we wouldn't have elected all those members."

He is taking far too much comfort from these results. Many westerners voted Tory only because the party had an attractive one-time issue – free trade – and because John Turner seemed to be no alternative as prime minister. Large chunks of the gigantic 1984 Tory vote slipped away to the New Democrats in British Columbia, Saskatchewan, and even Alberta, where the party elected its first federal member ever, Ross Harvey in Edmonton East. Donna Dasko of Environics feels that, without a free trade debate to unify the western Conservative vote, the next election could see a Trudeau-like collapse of Tory support in the region. Brian Mulroney made his best pitch to the West, perhaps the best he can ever muster, but westerners still haven't bought him.

A well-known humour columnist for the *Saskatoon Star-Phoenix*, Les MacPherson, nailed all these western perceptions of Mulroney with deadly accuracy in a "news item" he wrote for his column on June 22, 1989. Justly famous across the region, the column is often reprinted to renewed hoots of hilarity.

> OTTAWA – The federal government today announced it would award the Stanley Cup to Quebec, even though Alberta's Calgary Flames won the competition.
>
> The Cup will go instead to Quebec's Montreal Canadiens, who were defeated by the Flames four games to two in the

> best-of-seven series.
>
> Prime Minister Brian Mulroney said the hockey series was "only a guideline," and not binding. He conceded that Calgary might have the best hockey team, "but we have to look at what's best for all Canada."
>
> Mulroney said the decision to award the Stanley Cup to Montreal is based on Quebec's status as the traditional centre of hockey in Canada.
>
> "We have to support Canada's hockey industry, which is centred in Montreal,"said the prime minister. "Montreal is in the best position to take full advantage of the Stanley Cup."
>
> He said the decision to overrule the playoff results was "difficult and painful, but the national interest had to prevail over petty regional considerations..."
>
> Indignant Quebec MPs who lobbied long and hard for the Stanley Cup vehemently denied that the decision had anything to do with politics.
>
> "It's not as if the West isn't getting its fair share of federal support," sniffed Benoît Bouchard, the Tories' senior Quebec cabinet minister. "We've announced the Lloydminster upgrader eight or nine times. The West received the very lucrative contract for air in the CF-18's tires. And let's not forget about all that rain for western farmers this spring..."

After this appeared, the reaction at the newspaper was astounding. "The thing that amazed me was the number of people who thought it was true, that it actually happened," MacPherson said in an interview. "The thing was easy enough to write. I just went to the files, looked up what was said about the CF-18 decision, and changed a few words here and there." The simple technique pierced to the heart of westerners' attitudes about Mulroney and his government.

The prime minister professes not to mind all these regional rebuffs. "This is a business where they love you when you're gone," he said. "Western Canadians [will] only understand what a friend they had in Mulroney when there's someone else there." This makes him sound oddly vulnerable, like a scolded child who wants to run away so his parents will realize how much they miss him.

Will westerners love the prime minister when he's gone? Perhaps not, or if so, not for a long while. More than six years after the departure of Pierre Trudeau, many westerners still grind their teeth at the mere mention of his name. Some are still burned at Mike Pearson for the Canadian flag, and others are furious at John A. Macdonald for hanging Riel more than a century ago. Western love, once lost to a politician, is not an easy thing to recapture, but Brian Mulroney's smile tells us that he keeps hoping for a reconciliation.

FOUR

Bitter Allies

BY EARLY 1990, WESTERNERS WERE ANGRIER AT Quebec than they had been since the conscription crisis of the Second World War. Anti-Quebec outbursts were no longer limited to the so-called rednecks who have always resented and mistrusted Quebec. Now it was almost fashionable for westerners of all political stripes, from far right to the hard left, to vent their anger openly. Bilingualism was discredited even among westerners who once supported the idea of two official languages. Western politicians who still called for compromise – people like Saskatchewan premier Grant Devine and Alberta premier Don Getty – found themselves sneered at, ridiculed and buried at the bottom of the the opinion polls. Across the region, thousands cried "Let them go!" with never a thought to the consequences of Quebec independence, which are especially disastrous for the West.

These feelings were often based in a bitter belief that Quebec's grievances are always considered first, before those of the West. The long divisive debate on the Meech Lake accord aggravated this dangerous perception. The clear message to westerners from politicians was: We'll deal with Quebec first, and then you – maybe. Prime Minister Mulroney sent this signal dozens of times as he refused to consider any changes to the accord. The national premiers, including the westerners, flashed the signal as early as 1986, when they agreed at a meeting in Edmonton not to link their own provincial or regional demands to approval of a Quebec package. This might have worked if the Meech Lake accord, written in 1987, had quickly become law and talks on Senate reform had begun. But the wrangling that started when the Manitoba government changed in 1988 ensured that the simple message "Quebec first" would be repeated day after day, month after month. Westerners soon saw all the flaws in the accord, including its casual disregard of women, Natives, and the future of the Northwest Territories and the Yukon. Most of all they resented the refusal by Quebec and Ottawa to consider even the smallest improvements. They reacted furiously to the charge that they were wrecking the country by expressing their views. They condemned the very idea of eleven leaders meeting in private to write a constitutional deal for the whole country. A process that was supposed to unite the nation ended up dividing it further.

This was but one more sad episode in a long history of misunderstanding, both wilful and inadvertent, that has plagued Quebec and the West since before Confederation. The two regions should be each other's best friends in the country. (Often, at the political level, they are, because politicians recognize the natural links.) They share similar feelings of exploitation by Ontario and Ottawa, and this pushes them to struggle constantly for provincial rights to balance federal power. They also need each other to balance the influence of Ontario in the economy and political life. If Quebec and the West understood each other fully, were able to communicate more easily, were not so blinded by cultural differences, they could dominate the country together.

But their natural alliance is forever frustrated by language, history, and bursts of nervous diplomacy from federal politicians who fear the flowering of such a friendship. Federal actions often have a strange way of pushing Quebec and the West farther apart. This pattern is obvious in events that range from the hanging of Louis Riel in 1885 to today's constitutional bickering. The intention might not be malicious (although sometimes it is), but the result is always the same – a deeper chasm of mistrust between people who should be friends.

None of this should surprise anyone, given the peculiar historical relationship of Quebec and the West. Before Confederation they were only dimly aware of each other, and what they perceived was often depressingly wrong. Quebecers never really cared to settle the West, as historian A.I. Silver showed in his fascinating 1969 paper, "French Canada and the Prairie Frontier." For various reasons, some realistic and others wrong-headed, Quebecers considered the West to be Ontario's backyard – a notion that suited expansionist Ontario very well. Catholic missionaries, who at first discouraged settlement from Quebec, sent back bleak accounts of a hard life in a bitter land. Survival required "devotion that only Catholicism can inspire," wrote Alexandre-Antoine Taché, Archbishop of St. Boniface. Quebec missed its opportunity, the only one it would ever have, to create a roughly equal distribution of French and English speakers across Canada. The heroic French settlements pushed into the West by the early explorers and the Catholic church were left on their own to be overrun by pioneers from Ontario, Europe and the United States.

In the mid-nineteenth century, Quebec was already preoccupied with its own cultural survival. Governments of the day urged French Canadians to settle the province's northern frontier rather than stray to New England, Ontario or the West. "Colonization [of Quebec] thus seemed identical with national survival, with the maintenance of French Lower Canada," Silver wrote. "Colonization of another area – the North-West, for instance – was a contradiction in terms. To go to Manitoba was not to colonize; it was to emigrate, to abandon the *sol natal* [*sic*]."

With Confederation in 1867 this seemed even more imperative. Many Quebecers saw Confederation as a guarantee of Quebec nationhood, not as the founding of a broader country, and their first task was to build their own nation. After Manitoba became a province in 1870, its French leaders ran into a stone wall when they pleaded for migrants from Quebec. Political attacks on the French language and schools in Manitoba only reinforced the Quebec view that the new western country was poisonous to French culture. The execution of Riel confirmed this impression.

The Riel story follows the same pattern of uneasy alliance, betrayal and mistrust that today characterizes relations between Quebec and the West. Right from the beginning of the Riel Rebellion, many English-speaking settlers sided with the unhappy Métis in their agitation. The white Settlers' Union joined with the Métis in 1884 to write a platform listing all the grievances of the Saskatchewan region. "Support for the agitation was overwhelming," writes historian J.F. Conway in *The West*: "The press supported it initially and even the Prince Albert Tories toyed with the idea of adopting the platform as their own. The agitational meetings took on the character of a prairie fire, as they spread throughout the Saskatchewan territory and into the Alberta region."

The demands, Conway notes, were reasonable enough

and had been made many times before by both whites and Métis. They included better treatment for Indians, land settlement for the Métis, provincial status, representation in the federal Parliament, control of land and resources, vote by secret ballot, tariff reductions and a railroad to Hudson Bay. The enemy wasn't the Métis or the French language, but Ottawa and the Tory government of John A. Macdonald.

Riel's allies began to fade away, though, when he came back from exile in the United States. Armed insurrection – something Riel never wanted – loomed ominously. "Riel's arrival had already frightened the territory press, and many moderates among the white settlers, into silent neutrality, inactive sympathy, or open hostility," Conway says. "Only the bravest and most militant among the white settlers continued to support the movement. Even many English-speaking Métis had been scared off."

Riel begged the settlers: "Gentlemen, please do not remain neutral. For the love of God, help us to save the Saskatchewan." It was too late. The North West Mounted Police crushed the Métis and Indians at Batoche in May 1885. Riel was tried and convicted that summer, and Macdonald's cabinet denied the jury's plea for clemency. On November 16, Riel swung from the gallows at Regina. As the trap was sprung, the heavy sound of the body falling filled the air, and would echo for more than a century.

Macdonald had made good his brutal pledge that Riel would hang "though every dog in Quebec bark in his favour." Eight of the Métis leader's associates, all Indians, were also executed, but two white settlers were acquitted. This sealed for all time the bitter Quebec view that Riel's execution was grounded entirely on prejudice.

Today, its seems, Canada is irresistibly drawn every few months to hang Riel all over again, whenever there's a CF-18 decision, a debate on the Constitution or a dispute over language laws. Each time these poisons rise again, the bright hope of Riel's tentative alliances – between English and French, white and Native, Quebec and the West – sink deeper with him into his modest grave at St. Boniface. The headstone says simply, RIEL, 16 NOVEMBER 1885. The life speaks volumes about enduring bitterness between Quebec and the West.

It also sealed the fate of the Tory party in Quebec. Except for the brief Diefenbaker interlude, the Conservatives were punished there for ninety-nine years, until Brian Mulroney swept the province in 1984. Macdonald's blunders and misjudgements show that he hardly deserves his reputation outside Quebec as an all-wise founder of the nation. (At one point he said: "There is an attempt in Quebec to pump up a patriotic feeling about him [Riel] – but I don't think it will amount to much.") Macdonald embittered Quebec, helped poison relations between Quebec and the West by exploiting western linguistic and racial differences, and cynically used the affair to paint reasonable western grievances as unpatriotic. He killed the very alliances and friendships that could have made Canada a strong, vibrant, self-confident country in the twentieth century. Ultimately, he pleased only Ontario – a pattern westerners have noticed in many a prime minister since.

The legacy of this national tragedy still stands between Quebec and the West like a bloody curtain, blocking most perception of common interests. When Parti Québécois premier René Lévesque was abandoned by other premiers at the 1981 constitutional talks, many Quebecers saw him as a latter-day Riel, stabbed in the back at the moment of battle. Westerners, like the English-speaking settlers who supported Riel, found their Quebec ally useful to a point, but ultimately too radical to fully embrace. The very real differences between the interests of Quebec and the West shouldn't be underestimated; the tragedy is that, in any dispute, they inevitably overwhelm the vast area of common ground.

Despite all the bitterness, a political entente has often flourished, usually unnoticed by the national media. This intense Quebec-West relationship, at the level of bureaucrats and political leaders, is much stronger than most Canadians believe. The ordinary folk of Quebec and the West may live in their solitudes, but there is no silence or isolation between their leaders. When Alberta premier Don Getty lost his seat in the 1989 provincial election, Quebec's Robert Bourassa was one of the first to console him and urge him to run again. The same thing had happened to Bourassa, and the two men had recently done a very nice deal to limit minority language rights in their provinces.

Usually the mutual attraction for western and Quebec politicians is a belief in provincial rights – a credo every bit as ingrained in the western provinces as it is in Quebec. Sometimes it is a common dread of bilingualism at the provincial level. Always the magnet pulls against Ontario's influence, and Ottawa's need to define "national" interests that invariably offend half the country.

One official who worked for Alberta's Federal and Intergovernmental Affairs Department during the Lévesque era recalls how shocked she was when she realized there was a powerful bond between the Alberta and Quebec governments.

"Maybe I was naive, but I had no idea this link even existed. Right from my first meeting in Quebec City, though, I sensed the deep feeling between the provinces. The Quebecers really wined and dined us, treated us like true friends. Later on I realized that this alignment was based on a common respect for provincial rights and incredible mistrust of Ottawa and Ontario." Resentment over language was entirely absent, she recalls, even when it was a hot issue in the daily media. The officials got along very well – in English.

The alliance was certainly flourishing by 1978, when

René Lévesque came west to sell the notion of an independent Quebec. His message was that the West had nothing to fear from Quebec autonomy. The two regions had much in common, he told admiring audiences. At a reception after he spoke, Lévesque charmed everyone with his conversation, while downing most of a bottle of gin and smoking two packs of Players cigarettes. He made a lot of friends that day, including some influential people in the western governments.

In those days, with energy booming and Ottawa coveting the West's growing revenues, Lévesque's message fell on fertile soil. He expressed straight out the alienation and anger shared by many westerners. Lévesque became something of a western cult figure, liked and admired for his charm and respected for his courage in pushing his grievances to the limit. If this flirtation with Lévesque terrified Ontario and Ottawa, so much the better. He was the West's favourite imp.

And yet, the West did not buy Lévesque's main message. However sympathetic they were to Quebec alienation, separation was the last thing they wanted. Polls showed massive support in the West for compromise with Quebec. Westerners travelled to Quebec after the 1976 Parti Québécois victory to deliver huge petitions pleading with the province to remain in Canada. Lévesque failed in his main goal partly because westerners were so sympathetic and understanding. He would have done much better in today's western climate of hostility mixed with cold indifference.

Lévesque's western diplomacy was more than mere rhetoric; he delivered on the political level, too. He supported Peter Lougheed's drive for world energy prices at the very time Ontario was manoeuvring to keep prices low. Lévesque and the former Alberta premier were two of the first national leaders to endorse free trade. At every federal-provincial conference of the day, including the one that left

Quebec outside the Constitution in 1981, Lougheed had more in common with Lévesque than he did with Ontario's Bill Davis. The two men had very different goals, but they were united in a battle to wreck Ontario's overwhelming influence and limit Ottawa's authority, and sometimes they were very successful.

Yet this alliance of Quebec and western politicians is never any deeper than each leader's self-interest of the moment. It tends to operate only at the highest political levels, usually against powerful public stereotypes. This is a tricky game for the politicians. If they seem to be helping each other too much, they can find themselves in deep trouble with the public, especially when hostility runs high. Manitoba politicians took their long jump back from the Meech Lake accord in 1988 because their original support made them seem too soft on Quebec. Bourassa never admits in public that the West might have real constitutional grievances, even though he probably knows them by heart after years of hearing western premiers sound off in private meetings. Quebec premiers tamper at their peril with the cherished belief of Quebecers that only their province has a constitutional problem worth talking about.

Inevitably, these differences wrecked Lévesque's alliance with the West. He felt he was betrayed at the 1981 constitutional meeting when the other provinces signed an agreement that excluded Quebec. After several months of open, friendly alliance with other premiers, he seemed to have cause for anger. But the western leaders believed that a separatist would never sign even the most favourable deal. Whatever his motives, there's no doubt that Lévesque was truly angry. Lougheed says Lévesque didn't talk to him for two years afterward. "He wouldn't say a thing, he just looked away whenever we met," Lougheed recalls.

Years later, in 1988, the Quebec-West alliance was revived on a narrower issue by narrower men. The result was a remarkable sell-out of the rights of western francophones and Quebec anglophones by the premiers of Quebec, Alberta and Saskatchewan. The British Columbia and Manitoba leaders were bystanders at this show, but they weren't inclined to complain. After fighting a desperate battle for years to preserve their rights, French Canadians in the West suddenly realized that three provincial leaders were in charge of the result. This energetic little crew crushed forever the century-old French hope of fair treatment in Western Canada. By co-operating very carefully and skilfully, each premier gained power to dispose of the language minority in his own province just as he saw fit, without fear of criticism from the others. So effective was this entente that the premiers simply dismissed Ontario and Ottawa when they threw the language minorities overboard. They were in the pilot's seat and they knew it.

At first glance, the three premiers hardly seemed likely to co-operate on anything more ambitious than a long lunch at taxpayers' expense. Don Getty, Alberta's Conservative premier, was born in Westmount, Quebec, but by 1988 he was completely a westerner in his attitude toward the rights of the francophone community (not that such ideas were current in Westmount in his youth). His ideas were formed in the bum-slapping world of football, first at the University of Western Ontario in London, and then as a substitute quarterback for the Edmonton Eskimos.

Getty is a man of strong likes and equally powerful dislikes. He likes the guys in his own huddle, the thrill of winning everything with one long bomb thrown to the end zone, and friends who know he's not serious when he kids about violence. (Getty still can't comprehend why his casual joke about beating his wife and whacking his kids was taken so seriously in the 1989 election campaign, and helped cost him his own riding.) He likes watching thoroughbreds race at Edmonton's Northlands race track. He likes shooting ducks and tramping through the woods on Saturday afternoons. He is less impressed with people he considers to be unreasonable – leftists, journalists, or Alberta francophones who insist on full language rights.

Getty gets on fine with Saskatchewan premier Grant Devine, who succeeds very well in hiding an extremely quick mind. Although he's an agricultural economist with an M.A., M.B.A., and Ph.D., Devine talks like an aw-shucks hoser who's just about to spit tobacco over the next barn. At national events such as premiers' conferences, though, Devine is always dressed in expensive, well-cut suits and jackets. When the premier travels Saskatchewan in summer, he always keeps a baseball glove in the trunk of his car, just in case he spots a game. He's a good fielder who plays well to his government's rural base – and countryside Conservative voters in Saskatchewan are no lovers of French rights.

Compared to these two, Quebec's Robert Bourassa seems cold, hooded and bureaucratic, the very image of the urban Machiavelli. He learned his language politics in the cauldron of Quebec in the early 1970s, when the Parti Québécois was surging to power and intolerance was growing. Caught on the wrong side of Bill 22, which seemed too soft on English, the Liberal premier realized that one thing counts above all others in modern Quebec – pleasing the French-speaking majority. To learn that lesson, he endured Pierre Trudeau's abuse during the FLQ crisis. When Bourassa lost to Lévesque's Parti Québécois in 1976, he was the most hated Quebecer of his generation. By 1988, wiser, older and even colder, Bourassa was firmly back in power and determined not to be caught in the language trap again.

Bourassa certainly furthered this goal on April 12, 1988, when he came to Edmonton and held an amazing news conference with his friend Getty. The Supreme Court had just ruled, in the celebrated Mercure case, that Saskatchewan was still officially bilingual because the old Northwest Territories Act had never been replaced. In a province with a population of just over one million, where fewer than 35,000 people are of French origin and only 1 per cent of the people actually speak French from day to day, this came as a huge political shock. The court did add, though, that the province still had the right to pass a language law of almost any sort, either to preserve or to abolish bilingualism. In effect the judges gave the Saskatchewan Tories the authority to wipe out history at the stroke of a pen, or to show generosity and understanding of a rare and noble kind.

Although the case referred only to Saskatchewan, exactly the same historical and legal circumstances applied to Alberta. Until 1905, when both became provinces, Alberta and Saskatchewan were part of the Northwest Territories. The Alberta government said it accepted the result of the court case and promised to bring in a law, but shrewdly decided to let Saskatchewan act first.

Bourassa was on a trip to California when Saskatchewan brought down a bill that provided for translation of some laws, but left the unilingual character of the province intact. Nearly everyone expected Alberta's reaction to be even harsher. When the Quebec premier decided to go ahead with "commercial" visits to the premiers of B.C., Alberta and Saskatchewan, French speakers across the region hoped he would speak out strongly for their rights. They were to be cruelly disappointed.

Getty and Bourassa held a long, amiable meeting in the Alberta premier's office before they came into the adjacent cabinet room to meet reporters, including several from the Quebec City gallery who were travelling with Bourassa. Looking relaxed and comfortable, the premiers began talking about interest rates and the economy. They weren't about to discuss language if they could avoid it, but a few reporters soon asked the key question: What did Bourassa think of the new Saskatchewan bill?

Well, he believed it was just fine: it created some practical rights where none had existed before, he said (even though it abolished all the legal rights the court had recognized). On balance, Bourassa felt the Saskatchewan French were better off than they had been (although every French-Canadian leader had said this was a disastrous defeat). Clearly, he believed that limp privileges in practice are better than full rights in law. Bourassa expressed no sympathy for the *fransaskois* – the Saskatchewan francophones – and didn't even try to explain why his view was so radically different from theirs.

The old Quebec hands were astounded. Don Macpherson, the Montreal *Gazette*'s fine provincial columnist, shook his head in wonder. The French Quebecers looked stunned. One said it would be no exaggeration to call Bourassa a *vendu* – a sell-out.They were watching the end of a long and noble Quebec tradition that stretched back to Jean Lesage – the defence by Quebec, the *sol natal* of all French speakers in Canada, of French rights outside the province. Bourassa seemed to be casting western French Canadians adrift, once and for all, in the vast English sea.

Asked about the Alberta legislation to come, Bourassa said Premier Getty was perfectly able to protect the francophones in his own province. This was a remarkably trustful view, since the Tory Speaker of the Alberta legislature had recently condemned an MLA for merely asking a question in French. For months the Tory back-benchers had echoed with vindictive cries that the MLA, New Democrat Leo Piquette, apologize merely for speaking his own language. At the depth of this disgusting episode, somebody pinned a note to the legislature door demanding that Piquette return to Quebec. He declined, noting sadly that his family had lived in Alberta for generations – probably much longer than his tormentors. Piquette lost his seat in the 1989 provincial election, mainly because he had offended Natives in his northern riding by talking too much about French rights. The Tories put up a Métis candidate who beat him handily. Yet Bourassa seemed to think francophones could count on Getty and his MLAS for protection.

One of the most infamous examples of Alberta intolerance occurred in 1976, when a Tory back-bencher named Mick Fluker rose in the legislature to question a minister. He said: "I wonder if the minister is aware of the new seating capacity Mayor Drapeau has come up with for the Olympic Stadium."

The place fell silent with uneasy anticipation. Enjoying himself, Fluker continued: "I understand they are removing every other seat and are now replacing them with lily pads for frogs."

Some Tories laughed, but across the aisle Peter Lougheed, then the premier, was furious. He fired a note to Fluker and the next day the MLA explained that his remark had been a "joke." Afterwards, the legislators of all parties struck the remark from the official record; today it can be found only in newspaper accounts, a continuing blot on Alberta.

Fluker was hardly contrite. In a later campaign, when a voter asked him what he'd do for culture, he said: "I'd give a francophone to every Frenchman and a ukelele to every Ukrainian." But Fluker kept getting elected until he retired, in a sharply divided riding where 35 per cent of the voters are French.

In 1988, none of this seemed to bother Bourassa at all. The Quebec premier sat silently while Getty called the Alberta French "rude" for refusing to meet the distinguished visitor. (They feared that Bourassa had already betrayed them, since he had earlier cancelled a meeting with them in Quebec City.) Again, the Quebec reporters were astounded to see Bourassa stay silent while an English-speaking premier scolded francophones.

Altogether, it took about thirty minutes for the premiers to slight western French Canadians – and by implication, Quebec's English speakers as well. Both leaders denied they had any responsibility to defend language rights elsewhere in Canada. With a few shrugs and catch phrases, the efforts of previous Quebec premiers were trampled in the dust.

After more of the same the next day in Saskatoon with Devine, the French reporters following Bourassa were furious. Columnist Macpherson described how they went on "a two-day emotional binge.... They constantly disrupted news conferences with impassioned speeches in the guise of questions, or loud arguments with Bourassa's aides at the back of the room.... They so rattled Bourassa at his final news conference that several times he had to ask reporters to calm down. And they all but physically intimidated the spokesman for Saskatchewan francophones into finally giving them what they wanted." The reporters were content only when the *fransaskois* said Bourassa had betrayed them, and the francophones were certainly ready to oblige. One Quebec official told Macpherson they were "downright rude" during their private meeting with the Quebec premier. In the circumstances, they had a right to be.

The Alberta law, when it came down later, was even worse than expected. It made the province unilingual and threw only a few scraps to the francophones. In the legislature, MLAS would be allowed to ask their questions in French without prior permission, a move that raised the language slightly above the legal level of Pig Latin, but left it much the same status as other "ethnic" tongues. Bourassa didn't utter a word of complaint from Quebec City, even though Alberta had clearly broken its Meech Lake promise to preserve French in the province.

By that time Bourassa's true mission in the West was clear even to the most naive and trusting observers. He was buying western silence for his own impending language crisis, the Supreme Court decision on Bill 101. Bourassa had no interest whatever in protecting French rights anywhere but in Quebec. His goal was to purchase peace and silence at whatever price to minority rights.

The strategy worked brilliantly. Bourassa savoured his reward seven months later, after the Supreme Court ruled that Bill 101 violated the Charter of Rights, and he stepped around the decision by invoking the notwithstanding clause of the 1982 Constitution (this allows provinces to pass laws for five years even if they violate the Charter of Rights and Freedoms). Only Manitoba's Gary Filmon spoke out against Bourassa, not because of any burning fervour for French language rights, but because the Quebec drama gave him a heaven-sent opportunity to withdraw Manitoba's support for the Meech Lake accord.

As a defender of anglophone rights in Quebec, Filmon had about as much credibility as a cat in a bird cage. In 1983 his party spewed some of the vilest anti-French rhetoric of recent decades as it fought a Supreme Court decision ordering translation of provincial laws (very different historical circumstances applied in Manitoba – thanks to Riel – than in Alberta and Saskatchewan). Brian Mulroney, then the federal Opposition leader, responded with one of the great speeches of his career, an eloquent and passionate plea for national tolerance. But by 1988, Mulroney could not muster the political courage to apply the same tough standards to Quebec. The most bizarre outcome of this moral collapse is that Filmon became the strongest national defender of the English in Quebec. In the summer of 1989, he even wrote letters of support to Quebec anglophones who complained to him about Bill 178.

The other three westerners – Getty, Devine and Vander Zalm – had no quarrel whatever with Bourassa's action. (Bourassa had visited Vander Zalm, too.) Dave Russell, then

Alberta's deputy premier, stated the terms of the informal pact clearly when he said, "Quebec didn't comment on our [legislation], and we're not commenting on theirs." Bourassa made the same point in Saskatoon: "I would not like it if a premier from one of the other Canadian provinces came to Quebec and said, 'You should change section 4, you should modify section B, in one of my bills.'" They were voicing the true ethic of the Quebec-West understanding: Don't mess in our yard and we won't mess in yours.

And why should they interfere with each other? Bourassa was using a constitutional device dear to western hearts, one that grew on the premiers' own soil. The notwithstanding clause was the creation of three former western premiers: Conservatives Peter Lougheed of Alberta and Sterling Lyon of Manitoba, and New Democrat Allan Blakeney of Saskatchewan. Prime Minister Mulroney likes to blame Pierre Trudeau for this radical device, but in fact Trudeau was wary of the notwithstanding clause, and accepted it only after the provinces agreed to a five-year sunset provision. Trudeau sensed, correctly, that Quebec would use the clause to promote its language policies and autonomy, and he surely knew the West would eventually employ it to whittle away central authority.

Mulroney and the premiers could have tried to change this at Meech Lake in 1987, but they didn't bother. Most premiers liked the clause far too much to tamper with it. Only in 1989, after Quebec overruled the Charter and many Canadians grew concerned, did Mulroney suddenly see the dangers in the clause. He called for its abolition, but his chances for success are slim. Five provinces at least – Quebec, Alberta, Saskatchewan, Manitoba and British Columbia – are unlikely ever to agree. The clause serves their regional interests very well, and Quebec's action actually proved to them all just how useful the clause could be.

"Maybe Quebec did violate rights, but it probably prevented anti-English riots by doing so," said one western official privately. "Sometimes you have to weigh the benefits of public order against pure legal rights. In this case, the Quebec government knew what was best to preserve the social fabric. We like the section because it gives us this kind of flexibility too."

The saddest thing about the language debacle, perhaps, is that it perverted the useful Quebec-West alliance for a single, small-minded purpose. Most westerners were never aware of the reason their leaders remained silent while English rights were limited in Quebec. Ultimately, though, the plan backfired. Western anger with Quebec's Bill 178 was much deeper than the premiers expected, and it spawned the fierce regional reaction against Meech Lake. Devine and Getty spent much of the next two years trying to patch up an agreement they inadvertently helped to destroy.

They learned, perhaps, how dangerous it is to play recklessly with Canada's language demons. The western attitude to these problems today is as testy and explosive as it has been in a generation. Witness the strange case of a *Le Devoir* political cartoon, printed October 26, 1989, that caused roars of rage across the West, and especially in Manitoba.

The cartoon showed three figures wearing Ku Klux Klan robes while they burn Quebec's provincial emblem, the fleur-de-lis. The simple caption in French read: "Distinct society; Manitoba's intervention!" This was a reference to the all-party Manitoba report on the Meech Lake accord, which had just been released with demands for changes to the pact. The cartoon figures seemed to represent the three leaders whose parties wrote the report: Tory premier Gary Filmon, Liberal leader Sharon Carstairs and NDP leader Gary Doer.

When the cartoon was reprinted in western newspapers, many Manitobans were livid, and politicians quickly mounted their rhetorical podiums. "Cartoons coming out of Quebec do not help – looking at Manitobans as Ku Klux Klan members," fumed federal Energy Minister Jake Epp, a Manitoba MP. Filmon said: "For a government that has gleefully trodden on human rights, specifically the freedom of speech as guaranteed in the Charter of Rights and Freedoms, I don't think that they have any grounds to criticize anyone else." (Filmon was referring to Bill 178.) Doer called the cartoon "outrageous."

Carstairs happened to be in Montreal that day to meet the editorial board of *Le Devoir*. When editor-in-chief Paul-André Comeau refused to apologize for the unflattering depiction of Manitoba, the Liberal leader walked out in a great blaze of national publicity.

"I saw the cartoon that morning when it was passed to me at a press conference," Carstairs said in an interview. "I made the decision that there was no point having a discussion with people who had already decided that not I, but Manitobans, were racist.

"The Ku Klux Klan in Western Canada has taken on a very different meaning than in the United States – it's basically anti-French, anti-Catholic and anti-Semitic. I pointed that out to them. I said Manitobans are not racist, we're not anti-Semitic, we're not anti-Catholic, we're not anti-French. And there's not any point in me talking to you . . . if you're not prepared to recognize that and apologize for your cartoon.

"I am half French," the Liberal leader continued. "My mother's family, they're all Acadian. I'm a Catholic. To be painted that way, when two of those three things the Ku Klux Klan is [against] I happen to be, is personally offensive.... I have the walls at my office covered with cartoons. They can draw me any way they want and I get a big kick out of it, and I ask the artist for the originals and I frame them and put them on my walls. But this wasn't me. This was all

Manitobans. They wouldn't apologize, so I left."

In Quebec, many people seemed to be puzzled by the furious reaction to what was, after all, only a cartoon. Michel Vastel, the well-known Quebec columnist and radio commentator, thought he spotted a simple case of cultural misunderstanding.

"In the West you may not appreciate that for us, for Quebecers, the Klan is a kind of exotic image, the sort of thing you see in comic strips," Vastel said later. "We have never had a Klan, so we don't take it very seriously. I know the people at *Le Devoir* and I'm sure they did not want to give any such offence."

In the heat of this furious little debate, many Manitobans forgot an even more offensive cartoon that had appeared in the *Winnipeg Sun* in January 1989, during the dispute in Quebec over Bill 101 and its replacement, Bill 178. This cartoon also featured three figures: a Nazi storm trooper, a Klan member wearing robes and holding a noose, and a Quebecer with the number 101 written on his shirt, holding a match and a gas can. The caption said simply: "A history of cultural purists." Because the Klan truly is a powerful image in the West, the insult is correspondingly deeper and the *Winnipeg Sun* wins the war of bad taste hands down.

Carstairs said: "I was asked what I thought about that cartoon at the time and I said it was offensive." Doer was chastened when he saw the *Sun*'s cartoon months later. "At the time [of the Quebec cartoon] I did my ten-second clip and said the Quebec media was like *Pravda*. I guess I should say now that our own media can be homers too."

Another bizarre episode, also related to the Klan, shows that Manitobans were more concerned about criticism from Quebec than they were about images of home-grown intolerance. On this zany occasion, the Manitoba highways minister, Albert Driedger, actually shook hands with a group of men who wore hoods and carried burning torches.

It happened in Gladstone, a community of about 700 people located 140 kilometres west of Winnipeg, where many business people were upset about a provincial plan to reduce the number of parking spaces in front of their stores.

David McKinley, a local grocer, rounded up several friends to protest when Driedger came to town. They hit on the idea of wearing Klan-like hoods and carrying burning hockey sticks as torches. About six of them, with twenty or more town residents trailing behind, met the minister at an intersection. The *Winnipeg Free Press* reported that passing motorists honked their horns to show support, while others stopped to join the demonstration.

In an interview, McKinley insisted that his odd little parade had nothing to do with the Klan. "There's no way this was intended to offend anyone.... The thing was blown way out of proportion by the media. I've since watched those shows, *Cross of Fire* and *Mississippi Burning*, and there's nothing like that in Gladstone. Nothing!"

But some people were deeply offended, including Stephanie Karaz, who was then the mayor. "There were all these white pointed hoods and burning torches, and they just kept circling the building," she told the *Free Press*. "It was really scary." She said later in an interview with the authors: "If you want to demonstrate, fine. But don't pick the Klan."

The biggest surprise was the reaction of the highways minister, who seemed not the least put out. There's nothing wrong with wearing hoods and carrying torches, he said. "In fact, I mentioned to them we live in a country where freedom of expression is there. If they want to demonstrate, we don't hold that against anybody. If that's how they want to express their views, to me, that was fair enough."

Whether the episode was innocent or not, it was certainly much more unsettling than one cartoon in a Quebec newspaper. But Manitobans and other westerners weren't nearly as outraged by this peculiar event, somehow, as they were by that that single explosive picture from the other side of the language divide.

Frustration over official bilingualism, language laws, and Meech Lake doesn't begin to account for such western bitterness toward Quebec. Nor does the threat of separation. Today's anti-Quebec feeling is rooted in even more powerful grudges, including a deep sense of betrayal that brings the western centre-left – mainly New Democrats and Liberals – into alliance with angry western Conservatives, whose resentments are based mainly on language. Even western francophones are bitter because of the language-rights sellout by Quebec. For the first time in modern Canada, almost all segments of western society are in an anti-Quebec mood at the same time. This is a profound change from the days when at least one major group, usually the left, was willing to endure any amount of abuse to defend Quebec.

For western New Democrats and Liberals, the reason for anger is simple enough: they feel that Quebec was largely responsible for passage of the free trade agreement. Quebec stabbed them in the back, they say, after they had for many years supported conciliation, national unity, bilingualism – all the old buzzwords and devices that were supposed to make Quebec happy within Canada. Often they had to defend these policies against negative majority feeling in their own region, but they persevered out of deep affection, even love, for Quebec.

"The western centre-left was very accommodating toward Quebec," Gary Doer said in an interview. "The free trade thing really, really got them mad. I've always been very angry at the fact that we're now in an economic constitution with the United States to some great degree, because of the desire of Quebec to disentangle itself from an economic constitution with Canada.... I am emotional about free trade still."

New Democrats spent their time and treasure for years in futile efforts to make a breakthrough in the province. Former leader Ed Broadbent locked his whole national strategy toward the quest for that great elusive NDP Grail. His bilingual MPS, people like Lorne Nystrom and Michael Cassidy, stumped the province tirelessly before the 1988 election, vainly trying to show how much the party cared. There wasn't a single francophone in their caucus, and only Cassidy spoke really passable French, but they plugged away, hoping that sheer dedication would win the regard of Quebecers.

Between January and May 1986, Cassidy and Broadbent were each in Quebec nine times for press conferences, meetings with union officials and other public events. The whole NDP "Quebec group" – eight French-speaking MPS – made a total of forty-five appearances. New Democrats were more visible in Quebec, for those who cared to look, than even the resident horde of Tory government MPS.

For a brief time in the summer of that year, the strategy seemed to pay off; the NDP actually moved ahead of the Tories in the polls, 27 per cent to 20 per cent (although the Liberals were then far ahead at 48 per cent). Respectable commentators in Quebec began to imagine the inconceivable, that the NDP might actually win some seats.

Over the next two years Broadbent moved heaven and earth – although not his whole caucus – to protect these apparent gains. When the Meech Lake accord was signed in 1987, he was among its most loyal boosters, even though some of his western MPS went into revolt. (He removed B.C. member Ian Waddell from his critic's post when Waddell insisted on voicing his concerns.) Provincial NDP leaders in the West, including British Columbia's Michael Harcourt,

Saskatchewan's Roy Romanow, and Alberta's Ray Martin, had serious reservations about Meech Lake's failure to address the grievances of women and Native peoples. But they kept relatively silent because they were loyal to Broadbent – and because he might be right. If the party did win seats in Quebec, the problems with Meech Lake wouldn't seem nearly so serious. In politics – even NDP politics – nothing buries party grievances more deeply than success.

But Broadbent was proved wrong, because the Quebec gains were illusory. The 1988 election brought the party no seats in Quebec and only ten in Ontario, where the leader's Quebec stand was thought to be popular. The West and the Territories gave Broadbent thirty-three MPs – and a sharp lesson about where the NDP's real friends are.

Even during the campaign, western New Democrats were getting fed up with Broadbent's near-obsession with winning Quebec. Some felt that his fixation skewed his election strategy so badly that he missed out on the campaign's great issue, the free trade deal. When Liberal leader John Turner hit a national nerve during the TV debates by accusing Prime Minister Mulroney of selling out Canada, Broadbent seemed much milder. The NDP campaign stuck to its Bay Street versus Main Street campaign for days after free trade had become the major issue, and this allowed momentum to drain away to the Liberals. After the election, western New Democrats blamed the poll-oriented advisors around Broadbent. But in private, some wondered darkly if Broadbent hadn't played down the issue for fear of offending Quebec voters.

New Democrats are ever loyal to their leaders, however, so they preferred to blame Quebec for their disappointment. In Manitoba, Gary Doer moved quickly to withdraw his party's tentative backing for Meech Lake. He had always been uneasy about the deal, and after the election he saw no reason to contain his feelings. Mostly he was furious about Quebec's role in securing free trade.

"In Western Canada, people now perceive that it's Quebec's fault we've got free trade," says Doer. "The threat of separatism plus the free trade thing together – well, people just say, What's the sense of dealing with this issue if we're going to be threatened, and we're going to be dragged into an economic constitution with the United States anyway."

In Alberta, New Democrat Jeff Dubois, a francophone and a three-time candidate for the provincial NDP, was harsher still. "Stabbed in the back by Quebec again," he said on election night. "Well, screw 'em." For many western francophones on the left, the betrayal seemed deeper still when only weeks later Quebec set aside a Supreme Court decision in order to pass its restrictive language law.

Gordon Robertson, the former federal cabinet secretary who was Pierre Trudeau's chief advisor on federal-provincial matters for ten years, speaks eloquently about the misunderstanding and anger that persist today between Quebec and the West. "There is little comprehension in Manitoba, or in the West generally, of the concern in Quebec for the future of the French language and culture," he wrote in 1989 in a booklet called *A House Divided: Meech Lake, Senate Reform and the Canadian Union*. "Without that understanding, the 'language of signs' policy appears petty and vengeful: the method of imposing it, a confession of violation of individual human rights."

Westerners are used to such scolding from federal officials and they rarely like it, even from those raised in Saskatchewan. But Robertson sees the dark side of both regions. To him, Quebec's refusal to admit that the West has grievances against Confederation is just as distasteful and damaging.

Because of population and economics, he writes, "western interests and views, constantly in a minority in both Cabinet and Commons, receive little reflection in policy and no significant expression in the elected chamber of Parliament." Western constitutional dreams, especially, are dismissed as a "rural eccentricity: something of no consequence and deserving of no serious attention. Quebec's legitimate grievance of 1982 received prompt and energetic attention. The contrast has not been unobserved in the West. It adds to the frustration and irritation." And yet, Robertson adds, "thus far there has been no indication by the political leaders of Quebec of any awareness of legitimate constitutional problems anywhere else in Canada." With lofty irony, he notes that such recognition might be useful.

This is an understatement so vast that it could come only from a bureaucrat trained at Oxford. The truth is that such recognition might create an upheaval in Canadian politics. A Quebec-West alliance with full voter support, based on true mutual understanding and friendship, could be a powerful force for good in Canada. But the political leaders don't have the courage to reach for it. Instead, they prefer to forge their bonds quietly on limited issues of mutual benefit, as western francophones learned to their profound dismay.

We are left, mostly, with comic-book images of each other. When Quebecers think of the West at all, they are likely to visualize a vast rural hinterland of Ontario stretching in infinite boredom to the sea. There are no differences between Ontario and the West worth considering, they feel – even though the greatest part of the West is no more like Ontario than Quebec resembles, say, Moncton, New Brunswick. Westerners still see Quebec as a land of happy-go-lucky café dwellers who love to sing and dance, but lately there's a more damaging image too. Quebec politicians are thought to be a grasping, crooked gang who, with some exceptions, should go straight to the new patronage prison in the prime minister's riding.

In August 1989, events in Quebec City highlighted both the growing disenchantment and the cockeyed stereotypes that haunt these uneasy allies. As the ten premiers gathered for their annual national meeting, federal and provincial bureaucrats, some retired and some still active, assembled for a dinner and reunion. They included people with vast experience in forging links across the regions: Norman Spector, former federal-provincial expert in B.C., and now cabinet secretary in Ottawa for federal-provincial relations; David Cameron, special advisor on Quebec to Ontario premier David Peterson; Dr. Peter Meekison, former deputy minister for federal affairs in Alberta; Gordon Robertson; and many others. The private meetings were jovial, a bit like a class reunion, but the mood was not optimistic. For one thing, Claude Morin, once René Lévesque's federal relations mastermind, virtually snubbed the meeting, even though he lives in Quebec City. He attended only one dinner but avoided all the discussions. These talks left some of the participants seriously alarmed about the future of the country. "We went around the table," says Meekison, "and there was a consensus that Canada has a serious problem, a real national unity problem."

In public, on the fringes of the premiers' meeting, a very different show was going on; Bill Vander Zalm was showing how embarrassing he can be to any westerner who cares about Quebec. Not so much intolerant as sublimely insensitive to the impression he creates, the Socred premier of British Columbia is the image of a certain kind of westerner who blunders into Quebec with good intentions, but somehow manages to leave a shambles behind. It was small comfort that Vander Zalm is at least even-handed in his insensitivity: he also told Jewish jokes at the 1989 Socred party meeting that declared its devotion to "Christian principles."

The Quebec government put up the premiers at the marvellous Château Frontenac in the Old City. As they arrived one by one during the soft August evening, scores of journalists, American tourists and local rubberneckers watched the action. One American visitor, after hearing from reporters that Ontario's David Peterson was a Liberal, asked suspiciously: "Oh, is he one of those communists?" The throng was short on sophistication but eager for a show.

Enter Vander Zalm, who seemed determined to give them one. As he answered questions in a reporters' scrum about the federal proposal for a goods and services tax, the hot topic of the conference, he seemed less interested in the subject than in the action around him. In a few moments a most peculiar thing happened: a group of Quebec youngsters, apparently a visiting choir, began serenading Vander Zalm's wife, Lillian, with Quebec songs. The children were formed in rows on the steps, while Mrs. Vander Zalm listened with delight in front of them, and the tourists stopped to watch.

This was too much for the bouncy premier, who can never resist a chance to sing, perhaps because British Columbians seemed to love his remarkable melodic outbursts during the 1986 election campaign. He suddenly bolted from the scrum, leaving reporters to lurch after him with their notebooks and microphones. To the surprise of the children, he stepped into the back row of the choir, wiggling his shoulders a bit to make a place for himself. Some of the singers looked up at him as if he might be the sort of fellow their parents warned them about. Then Vander Zalm began to lead them – or tried to – with a bellowing chorus of "Alouette."

The children looked lost; they hardly seemed to know the words. Quebec reporters gaped with astonishment. "My

God," one said later, "that's like going to Mississippi and singing 'Old Man River' with the black people. Nobody sings that song here anymore." A reporter from Regina added: "Now all we need is some real western culture – maybe Grant Devine can come out and lead them in a round of 'Turkey in the Straw.' "

It was a small thing, really (although it would have been much bigger if the TV cameras had been there to record it). The Quebecers didn't seem to take any particular offence, perhaps because they don't expect anything better from westerners. We are not supposed to understand them, not really, so why should we behave any differently? Vander Zalm just smiled, believing that everyone was having a wonderful time there in Qwe-bec. One westerner on the spot expressed relief that Vander Zalm hadn't made a real blunder, perhaps by asking his hosts if the Plains of Abraham has anything to do with the Israeli Air Force.

Such episodes suggest that novelist Hugh MacLennan's famous phrase, two solitudes, no longer begins to describe the vast gulf of misunderstanding that divides Quebec and Western Canada. These regions have gone a long way down their separate roads – much too far – since the early days of the Riel Rebellion, when Quebec and the West cheered the Prairie hero with almost equal enthusiasm. They hardly recognize any more that they share a long fellowship of alienation that should draw them closer together. Instead, westerners and Quebecers focus on differences that drive them ever farther apart. If there's a serious danger signal for Canada in the 1990s, this is it.

Many westerners now think it's time to wave goodbye to Quebec forever. Across the four provinces, across party lines, across even the French-English divide in the West, people say: "If Quebecers want out, let them go!" Such statements, once whispered only by right-wingers, are now respectable. They come from New Democrats, Liberals and

Tories, lawyers and labourers, farmers and city dwellers. Few westerners seem to realize that Quebec independence could make their worst fear come true.

"Let's say Quebec does go," argues Peter Meekison. "You've got 25, 26 million people in the country, and Quebec takes a quarter of them out. If you look at the rest of the country, Ontario has just about half. With Quebec going out, we'd turn control of the country over to Ontario.

"You know, there is this community of interest between Quebec and the West that is one of the balancing mechanisms against Ontario. Take that mechanism out, and people in Western Canada will realize, my God, that's terrible. And then you'd see the bonds of Canada really slipping, and we'd all gravitate toward the United States in 25 years." Nothing makes this drift toward breakup more likely than the enduring lack of empathy between Quebec and the West.

FIVE

Love That Hinterland

FOR MANY WESTERNERS, ONTARIO IS A LOFTY, remote presence that dominates national politics, controls their economic fate, harbours the villainous chartered banks, yet seems blithely unaware of western anger. Toronto is all the power of Ontario distilled and refined into one pulsing giant, the city that swallows everything the West wants and needs. The irritants range from large national disputes over resource control to smaller everyday problems. Waiting for that special-order bathtub for your Vancouver renovation? Sorry, a store in Toronto bought the whole production run. Is the most recent bestseller late arriving at your little Regina bookstore? Too bad, the Toronto publisher sent every copy to the hot Southern Ontario market. Western retailers tell similar horror stories about furniture, appliances, cars and many other products made in Ontario. Toronto comes first, the West gets the leftovers – maybe.

Westerners at least used to be able to kid Toronto in the puritanical days when it was Toronto the Good. After moving there from Calgary in 1909, Bob Edwards wrote: "Compared with a Toronto Sunday, the Scottish Sabbath is a French ball." Suffocated, the hard-drinking journalist fled Toronto within weeks. Today westerners are forced to concede that Toronto is a vibrant, exciting metropolis, even if the prices are so absurd, and the traffic so hellish, that no sane person would really want to live there. They joke about Toronto's claim to be "world-class," but after a visit, they quietly agree that it just might be true. And they carefully measure their own cities against the Ontario powerhouse.

Toronto is also the home of the Ontario government, the most troublesome crowd next to Ottawa, the bunch that often seems to dangle the federal government from puppet strings. Queen's Park, sitting smugly at the edge of the financial canyons, is the only legislature in Canada where provincial politicians believe they speak for the whole country. Queen's Park has brewed plenty of trouble for the West over the years; support for the National Energy Program was hatched there, and so was the Ontario government's backing of Prime Minister Trudeau's first constitutional package. A century ago, Ontario politicians in these neighbourhoods called for the blood of Louis Riel and argued for settling the West as a captive market. Yet Ontarians always seem puzzled when they encounter western anger, which comes out in some very peculiar ways.

The huge crowd that lined the route of the Calgary Stampede parade on July 7, 1989, was in a fine mood, ready to cheer for almost anything. The summer weather was glorious and the city was prospering after several years of struggle in the mid-1980s. The parade was the most spectacular ever – a good-natured procession of bands, floats, horses, cowboys, Indians, and even a shepherd with his dogs and a small flock of hyperactive sheep. It seemed that nothing could sour this throng.

Suddenly a curious stillness fell over the crowd. A float was coming – a big one, with several people on it, all of them madly waving and smiling into the vast silence. It was the Metro Toronto entry. COME TO GREY CUP '89 IN TORONTO, it said. Hardly anyone smiled or applauded; instead, the Torontonians were rewarded with a chilly calm, punctuated with a few startling boos. The reaction couldn't have been cooler if Pierre Trudeau had appeared on a horse to give his famous one-finger salute to the West.

But then another reaction set in. People looked at one another sheepishly, embarrassed at the crude treatment of a visitor, one who had clearly gone to a lot of trouble for this event. The booing was a shocking violation of the code of western hospitality. A smattering of applause began, followed by a few restrained cheers. Soon the Torontonians were treated to a full, friendly western greeting. This was a wonderful day, the opening of the world famous Calgary Stampede, so why not be generous to the tinhorns?

The episode revealed so many western feelings about Toronto and Ontario; the resentment, the anger, the misunderstanding – all the feelings that get so much bad publicity – but also the persistent western desire to make things right, to begin at last to deal with each other as equals, to put the bad blood and suspicion behind us. Westerners sense that this day is a long way off, but most of them care enough about the country to yearn for its arrival. And they long for signs that Ontario cares as much.

These emotions are perhaps most powerful in Calgary, the western city that always seems most annoyed by Toronto, and that inspires equally strong feelings among Torontonians. Calgary and Toronto are more alike than they realize; both are cities of strivers, eager to dominate their territory, almost desperate to be known as "world-class." After winning its long commercial struggle with Montreal, Toronto is clearly the giant of Central Canada and the most powerful city in the country. Calgarians burn for the same leading role in the West and beyond (although they rarely admit it). No other western city is so ambitious and aggressive. Vancouver, although much larger, is content just to be where it is. Its dreamy ambitions focus on Asia and the United States' West Coast rather than the rest of Canada. Winnipeg rules Manitoba but strives for little else. Regina is simply too small to reach beyond Saskatchewan, and Edmonton tends to be insular and self-contained. Only Calgary shows a flash of Toronto's imperial quality. If Calgarians can't control more territory, they will always try to grab something: media attention, sports championships, as much commerce as they can find. With the Rockies rising gloriously in the west, and the vast plain stretching away endlessly to the east and south, the horizons are limitless and everything seems within reach. This is perhaps why Calgary often plots and plans when other westerners complain and stew (although Calgarians can certainly complain with the best when the urge strikes). And Toronto, recognizing a rival much like itself, reacts with gut hostility to Calgary's upstart ambition.

Even as the Stampede parade snaked its way through downtown Calgary, one of these irritants was about to erupt into an unpleasant round of name calling between the two cities. The Toronto Humane Society had announced its opposition to a scheduled 1990 appearance by the Stampede in Toronto's Skydome, alleging that the show thrives on cruelty to animals. Calgarians were stunned by this rebuke. During the controversy, which lasted for months, one Toronto alderman compared the Stampede to the "gladiators of ancient Rome." In a formal report, the city's medical officer of health condemned rodeos. Councillor Nadine Nowlan complained: "I can understand the Calgary Stampede in the cultural context of the Wild West, but it's quite contrary to our whole history and tradition." Predictably vexed, the *Calgary Herald* expressed the city's outrage in an editorial that returned insult for insult: "Serious elements are protesting that Stampede rodeo events amount to animal cruelty and are not part of Toronto's heritage. They are half right. Rodeos are not part of the history of Hogtown and southern Ontario sodbusters. Their ancestors' tastes ran more to bearbaiting and cockfights."

The Stampede board finally cancelled the tour with the full support of most Calgarians. Given the depth of anger and misunderstanding on both sides, this was just as well. Torontonians wouldn't recognize a horse if a palomino trotted in their quiche, Calgarians snorted. Barbarians, Toronto retorted, don't they know what century this is?

Toronto might have a point about rodeo cruelty; many westerners worry about this too, although Stampede officials insist that the animals are treated like kings. But rejecting the Stampede, with its ethic of flat-out fun and hospitality, was equivalent to stomping on Calgary's very identity. Some Ontarians were more sensitive, of course. Toronto mayor Art Eggleton appeared quite understanding during the dispute, and a top official in the Ontario government told the authors that "a pack of nuts" have taken over the Toronto Humane Society. "They're all weird," he said. But once again, many westerners felt that Toronto was displaying its familiar casual ignorance of their traditions.

In 1989, TransCanada PipeLines decided to move its headquarters from Toronto to Calgary, and tried to convince some 720 employees to make the move. But a company questionnaire revealed stunning misconceptions about the western city. Some workers wondered if Calgary has an organized hockey system, if there is a university nearby, and if French immersion is available in the schools. Calgarians were amazed to realize that some Torontonians actually hadn't heard of the Calgary Flames (then the Stanley Cup champions), the respected University of Calgary, and one of the highest rates of immersion schooling in the country. Vastly understating the obvious, Calgary mayor Al Duerr said: "It shows we have a real selling job to do . . . to many who must have felt they were at the centre of the world and didn't feel the need to look beyond their own boundaries."

Unfortunately, Duerr came up with a typical western response to the problem. In January 1990, the mayor led a delegation to Toronto to convince the TransCanada Pipe-Line workers that Calgary is really a cosmopolitan place, a kind of Paris with cowboys. "Yes, cowboys and cow punching are an important tradition for Canada and the West," Duerr said. But after the annual Stampede, "a lot of the cowboy boots are put away and the Giorgio Armani suits go on." This caused some head scratching among many Calgarians who had never heard of the Italian designer or his suits. But the Calgarians went to Toronto, with some librarians in tow, to show that westerners can read. Duerr even managed to apologize for former mayor Ralph Klein's statement, made in 1982, that Calgary had to protect itself from eastern "creeps" and "bums." Duerr offered: "I think the city was a little immature at the time." But it was Lanny McDonald, the former Toronto Maple Leaf turned Calgary Flame, who best expressed the spirit of this venture. "We're not downgrading Toronto," he insisted, "we're just trying to show them we're not out in the boonies."

Only Calgary, the runaway champion of western boosterism, could mount such a rah-rah enterprise. This is the same admirable quality that won for the city the 1988 Winter Olympics and then produced the warmest, friendliest Games in anyone's memory. But the Toronto trip also exposed the deep sense of inferiority that endures throughout the West and seems especially transparent in Calgary. The tip-off was Duerr's assertion that Calgarians aren't cowboys, not really, even though cattle and cowpokes made the town, and Calgarians proudly celebrate this plain fact year after year. Today it's only a show for the tourists, the mayor implied. To make the point quite clear, nobody from the Stampede board was invited along on the Toronto jaunt (although some on the board say there was a last-minute invitation). This brought an explosion from Calgary alderman Ron Leigh, who raged: "What the hell are we afraid of? What are we ashamed of? I think this is an insult for the 1,500 volunteers who make the Stampede click every year."

The Toronto media had great fun with the visit. The *Toronto Star*, ever eager to spot straw behind western ears, observed with glee: "Instead of cowboy hats and hayseed, Calgarians yesterday were sporting leather loafers and silk ties and bragging about their ballet and theatre." In an editorial titled "Sushi at the Rodeo," the paper said Duerr had "repackaged Calgary as a kind of Metro with Mountains, a place where ballerinas need not worry about dirtying their slippers beside the hitchin' post."

It's hard to imagine Toronto making a similar pilgrimage to the West or anywhere else in Canada. Would the Ontario capital deny any part of its heritage, even the Mafia, to impress westerners? Not likely. Toronto these days seems more concerned about wowing outsiders such as New York and Los Angeles with its new status as an international player.

Duerr dove into the soup again in February 1990, when he visited Quebec City's winter carnival during the dispute over Ontario cities and towns declaring themselves unilingual. Like most westerners, the mayor was eager to make the point that his home isn't cluttered with bigots. So he said: "People say Calgarians are rednecks and right wing, yet we are much less so than you would find in Ontario." Ontario's actions showed a clear lack of tolerance, he suggested.

The Ontario comeback was quick and hot. Toronto's Mayor Eggleton, his own tolerance snapping, shot back: "They've got their share of rednecks." He added, quite correctly, that no province is blameless. Mel Lastman, the North York mayor who is always proud to take a pop at Alberta, was even more blunt. "Every mayor from Calgary makes his mark by making stupid, dumb remarks," Lastman crowed. "You've got to excuse them. Ralph Klein was just as dumb when he was elected."

Predictably, Duerr apologized, thus becoming the only western mayor in recent memory to beg Ontario's forgiveness both for his predecessor and for himself. "If there was any offence taken, I'll apologize for that because there was no intent to slur Ontario generally," he said. In the end, the mayor was roped and hog-tied by the power of the Ontario media to create a national stereotype overnight.

Yet when casual insults pop out of Ontario, even true whoppers, there is rarely any apology. The absolute classic, the offensive remark to top them all, came from Don Blenkarn, the Tory MP for Mississauga South and chairman of the Commons finance committee. No delegation has yet appeared to explain that he didn't mean what he said, and westerners will likely wait for an apology until Winnipeg replaces Ottawa as the nation's capital.

In October 1989, Blenkarn made a mind-numbing gaffe while responding to a rising western revolt against the proposed goods and services tax. After his committee was blasted by citizens at a raucous meeting in Edmonton, the blunderbuss MP said: "I fail to understand how the level of education can be so low in the community. I guess what we ought to do is send a bunch of grade five school teachers out here. I've never seen such stupidity in all my life. I wonder what they are, out to lunch or what."

Blenkarn hit a button guaranteed to propel the whole West into orbit. *Edmonton Journal* columnist Rod Ziegler voiced the general view when he wrote: "The Commons Finance Committee and the Moscow Circus hit town Wednesday. It was impossible to tell them apart." Open minds on the tax question slammed shut, and by the time Blenkarn headed back East, not noticeably chastened, the federal proposal was in worse shape than ever. (Hardly anyone seemed to recall that westerners had applauded Blenkarn a year earlier when his committee attacked the fees charged by chartered banks.)

When Blenkarn returned for a speech some weeks later, he was hanged in effigy on the back of a flatbed truck. Columnist Ziegler, ever a keen observer of wacky western detail, reported that the advertising flyer for the demonstration said: "Street Rally! We won't pay Don Blenkarn's GST. Come Watch the Fun. Come See Blenkarn Hang!!! (Effigy) Be on TV!" The radical Western Independence Party was behind this, but nobody bothered to defend Blenkarn.

He had managed to offend a very wide range of people who usually despise each other. These included Alberta treasurer Dick Johnston, Reform Party leader Preston Manning, Alberta Federation of Labour president Don Aitken, other union leaders, and many more. Prime Minister Mulroney handled this tempest fairly well by making a joke of it. Even westerners had to laugh when the prime minister said of Blenkarn: "You should hear what he calls me!" And yet, Mulroney didn't really chastize Blenkarn or make any move to silence him, at least not in public. This left the damaging impression that Mulroney did not entirely disagree with his MP's remarks.

This pattern of western anger and apology, resistance and submission, shows the true power relationship of Ontario to the West. Westerners still sense that they are colonials and behave accordingly, even when they hate themselves for doing it. Ontarians often regard the West as their "hinterland," and thus reveal an imperial lack of concern for the feelings and interests of the colonials. It's no coincidence that the Prairie West was settled with the British imperial model in mind; it was to have the same relationship to Ottawa and the existing provinces as Canada had to Britain. As Donald Swainson explained in *Canada Annexes the West*: "During the 1850s, a dynamic and expansive Upper Canada saw the North-West as its proper hinterland. It was regarded as a huge extractive resource, designed to provide profit for the businessman, land for the farmer, and power for Toronto." By changing only the date and a few archaic words, a westerner can apply that description to Canada during the battle over the National Energy Program only ten years ago.

George Brown of the Toronto *Globe* was one of the chief colonial crusaders, and he brought a truly imperial zeal to his dream of settling the West. "[Canada] is fully entitled to possess whatever parts of the great British American territory she can safely occupy," he wrote. "Possess" is the operative word. Brown didn't see the West as a new partner in Canada, but as a tool to further Ontario's goals, including the expansion of commerce. Westerners still receive traces of Brown's Ontario paternalism six days a week by satellite in the *Globe and Mail* .

This feeling of ownership persists in Ontario today, and very often the people who hate it the most are Ontarians who have moved and put down new roots in the West. After being told in their youth that all Canadians are first-class and equal, these former Ontarians discover that their political power is suddenly diminished because they live in the West. In their resentment, they can be as fierce as hungry coyotes. As Premier Peterson says, with considerable exasperation, "Some of the toughest, rottennest, meanest westerners I know are guys who moved out there from here a year ago." These are the people who will buttonhole an Ontarian on holiday, poke him in the chest, and tell him how Ontario is screwing the rest of the country. Such encounters don't do much for western tourism, but they show how people resent being denied the political power they enjoyed in Ontario – especially when they find it being used against them.

Modern western leaders have spent an enormous amount of time and energy trying to limit Ontario's massive influence on the nation, and especially on federal policy. By the 1960s and early 1970s, western premiers were determined to break the old pattern of federal decision-making. This process often consisted of a few consultations with Ontario and Quebec, and then a federal announcement that would come as a complete surprise to western premiers. The classic example was the introduction of the Canada Pension Plan in 1966. Ottawa struck a separate deal with Quebec, made sure Ontario had no objection, and then revealed the details to the rest of the provinces. There were really three senior partners in the country – Ottawa, Ontario and Quebec – and eight junior ones.

This collusion, especially between Ontario and Ottawa, was galling to western leaders. Peter Lougheed likes to tell a story about how he watched in amazement as Bill Davis, then the premier of Ontario, interrupted a national premiers' meeting in 1974 to pass messages to the federal government. "I was astounded," Lougheed says. "He would look around and say, 'Have you got that?' or 'Make sure Pierre hears about that, will you?'" Only later did Lougheed learn that Davis was talking to Tommy Shoyama, then the deputy finance minister in the Trudeau government, who was sitting with federal observers. The next year, Lougheed demanded that federal officials be excluded from the premiers' meetings. The other leaders agreed, and the federal troops haven't been seen since at the annual gatherings (even though the premiers still gladly use the Canadian Intergovernmental Conference Secretariat, a body funded by Ottawa and the provinces, which provides organization and simultaneous translation).

Western hostility toward Ontario was never deeper than it became in the 1970s and early 1980s, when oil and gas prices rose sharply with the OPEC cartel's control of the world market. Ontario's simple interest was to keep prices low (although the provincial government always talked about the "national" interest). Many westerners felt that the producing provinces should get full benefit from a short-term boom in a resource they owned under the Constitution. Quebec, citing the principle of provincial control, sided strongly with the West on resource issues, even though this stand did not favour the interests of Quebec consumers. The Atlantic provinces, as buyers of offshore oil, were a smaller political factor, although Newfoundland under Brian Peckford ardently supported the western producers. New Brunswick's Richard Hatfield was also sympathetic. But in this fight the battle order was clear; it was western producers versus Ontario consumers, a basic tension of Confederation starkly etched for all to see.

If the struggle itself was for heroic stakes, the day-to-day skirmishes were often petty. In the West in the late 1970s, cars with Ontario licence plates drew traffic tags with suspicious frequency. A vehicle parked in Edmonton, one of Canada's flattest cities, got a ticket for being "illegally parked on a hill." The owner, a migrant from Ontario, took the hint and bought his Alberta plates the same day. Ontarians who moved to the West (and many thousands did) were subjected to regular harangues until they came around to the proper view. In 1979, Don Getty, then Alberta's energy minister, accused a questioner of being "un-Albertan" at a public meeting. The man had merely asked whether Alberta's energy policy was actually written in stone by a divine finger.

Ontarians were no less adamant. Newspapers regularly berated the western oil sheiks as un-Canadian. One western journalist, visiting the editorial page editor of the *Toronto Star*, was amazed to hear the man say that Ottawa should send in the troops if Alberta continued to resist. During the 1980 federal election campaign, Stuart Smith, then the leader of the Ontario Liberals, told a cheering crowd at Toronto's Royal York Hotel that "Peter Lougheed has to learn he can't be a member of OPEC and a member of Canada at the same time." Sitting beside him, smiling faintly, was the man who would later try to teach the lesson: Pierre Trudeau.

The 1970s had begun with little sign of these hostilities. After Lougheed was first elected on August 30, 1971, he went to Ontario and campaigned with Davis in the Ontario election. In those innocent days before the energy price explosion, western and Ontario leaders could exchange public compliments without destroying each other's careers. But by 1973, Ontario's resistance to rising gas prices brought the collapse of this cosy Conservative cabal. On April 3 that year, Premier Davis warned in Calgary that Ontario industry could not absorb the cost of higher prices. "If price changes must come, they must be sufficiently gradual to enable consuming industries to adapt," he told the Canadian Petroleum Association. Raising the Ottawa hammer once again, the deceptively avuncular premier warned that co-operation would be better than unilateral action by the federal government.

Earlier that day, Davis had met Lougheed privately for a half-hour exchange at Edmonton International Airport. They traded tough words, with Lougheed insisting that Alberta's resources wouldn't be sold below fair value, and Davis stressing the danger to Ontario industry. Lougheed realized then that there was little room for compromise. Their earlier friendship, based on Tory camaraderie and commiseration over old football injuries, started to cool noticeably. In the fall, the Trudeau government moved to stop the rise in oil prices and to skim off some of the revenue flowing to Saskatchewan, Alberta and British Columbia. It imposed a price freeze, slapped an export tax on oil sold to the United States, and denied oil companies the right to deduct provincial royalty payments when calculating their federal taxes.

In 1975, the Saskatchewan government tried to nationalize part of the potash industry, but the federal government dragged the province through the courts. With the full approval of Ontario, Ottawa was systematically denying the western provinces the full control of resources supposedly guaranteed by the Constitution. Davis enjoyed the advantage of watching Ottawa carry out policies nicely tailored to Ontario's needs.

Of course, not all westerners felt equally oppressed, and western leaders didn't always agree on tactics. When Dave Barrett was the NDP premier of British Columbia from 1972 to 1975, he refused to blame Ontario for arguing its local interests in energy policy. "I stayed out of the Ontario-bashing by Peter Lougheed," Barrett said in an interview shortly after his 1989 loss to Audrey McLaughlin in the federal NDP leadership race. "I didn't see it that way. I saw it from a pan-Canadian perspective. I felt that as a nation we had to better secure our own oil and gas supplies for our own needs, and not have them dictated by the oil industry.... Ontario had its own agenda, as well as Alberta. I had my own too. I did not get into Central Canada-bashing on that issue, although I did it sometimes, on other ones. Oil and gas are more important to the nation than to any single province. When I said this, I tell you, I found myself arguing all alone."

Barrett often alarmed his western colleagues with centralist ideas they considered wild and dangerous. At one point, he actually proposed that Ottawa be allowed to manage all oil and gas resources as a public utility. Under this plan, private companies would develop the reserves and the federal government would control them in the public interest. When he proposed this at an energy conference, Barrett recalls, Lougheed sent him a private note that concluded: "This is where I leave you, buddy."

"I said that if they [Ottawa] would assure that the marketing profits be returned to the public coffers, I would have given up ownership," Barrett remembers. "I would have campaigned on it in our own province, saying 'We are all Canadians.'" The NDP's defeat by Bill Bennett's Socreds in 1975 suggested powerfully that many British Columbians didn't like Barrett's ideas, but there's no doubt that he represented a great many voters on the Lower Mainland, if not in the province's more conservative interior.

In Saskatchewan, NDP premier Allan Blakeney was much more wary of both Ottawa and Ontario. He and Lougheed, the Alberta Tory, usually co-operated on tactics, and when they didn't, each kept the other informed about what he intended to do. If their solutions to the energy dilemma weren't always identical, they did share a powerful suspicion of Ontario. "We had a pretty solid understanding about what was going on," Blakeney said in an interview from Toronto, where he is a visiting professor of law at Osgoode Hall. "It seemed to us that now that some other province was threatening to become as wealthy as Ontario, it was time to distribute the wealth. I used to say in those days, 'We'll distribute it, but there will be a certain time-lag. Come back in about eighty years and we'll discuss it.' That's about the period we had to wait to benefit from our resources. They [Ottawa and Ontario] tried to highly selectively change the rules, but not for all resources."

Blakeney recalls that Ottawa challenged provincial ownership of offshore oil in Atlantic Canada, but had no quarrel with Ontario's ownership of gas wells in Lake Ontario. Where Ontario is concerned, there seems to be legal magic even in fresh water. The former premier sees little prospect of change. "If you view Canada as a country designed with a colonial hinterland to provide for the heartland," he argues, "you are not going to get any agreement on distributing power or wealth to the hinterland. This would stop the even flow of money to Toronto."

Manitoba's role in these debates was often less clear, partly because the province is so divided between western instincts and centralist interests. With the most diverse economic base in the West, and a common border with Ontario, Manitobans are often pulled toward the centre (even the province's football team, the Winnipeg Blue Bombers, has been in the eastern division of the Canadian Football League for years). Sterling Lyon, the Tory premier from 1977 to 1981, backed Lougheed to the limit in his battles with Ontario and Ottawa. This was a dangerous thing to do in a province with no oil and gas worth mentioning. Just as Barrett offended British Columbians who mistrusted Ottawa, Lyon annoyed Manitobans who were worried by the new wealth in Saskatchewan, Alberta and British Columbia. And, like Barrett, he lasted only one term.

The NDP premiers who held office before and after Lyon – Ed Schreyer and Howard Pawley – were much friendlier to Ottawa and Ontario. Schreyer was an unabashed advocate of strong central power, which is surely one reason Trudeau made him Governor General in 1979. Manitoba can be as furiously western as any of the other provinces when it is visibly shafted by Central Canada. But in the great battle over energy, it was an unreliable ally for the producing provinces.

The conflict between Ontario and those provinces, usually muted by Ottawa's role as biased referee, burst into the open when Joe Clark was minority prime minister from May 22, 1979, to February 18, 1980. Clark's strategy, to raise prices gradually to world levels, terrified the Ontario government. Suddenly unable to count on help from Ottawa, Ontario had to join the struggle directly, and this led to a monumental confrontation between Davis and Lougheed.

It exploded on August 14, 1979, on the eve of a premiers' conference held in Pointe-au-Pic, Quebec. Just before Davis left Toronto for the meeting, he revealed a plan for sharing petroleum revenues equally among consumers across the country. Davis intended to use oil profits in a "national energy and employment adjustment program." While continuing to oppose a scheduled $1 a barrel increase for oil, he argued that any price hike beyond that amount would have "horrendous" effects on Canada's economy and, ultimately, on Confederation itself. If a solution couldn't be negotiated, he suggested, Ottawa should simply impose one. In effect, Davis wanted an emergency declaration that oil is a national resource, not a provincial one. And he was calling for direct federal intervention against the producing provinces.

Lougheed, in Montreal en route to the conference, was startled by the ploy. He had expected something like this but the early release caught him off guard. The premier ordered his deputy minister for Federal and Intergovernmental Affairs, Dr. Peter Meekison, to draft a detailed reply. Meekison burned up the phone lines to Edmonton for most of the night, and by the next day a six-page document was ready. Suitably armed and ready for action, the warriors from both sides headed for one of the most dramatic premiers' meetings in the history of these events. Former prime minister John Diefenbaker died while the sessions were on, and a tremendous fuss erupted when the Parti Québécois government of Quebec forgot (or deliberately neglected) to lower flags. A boat intended to ferry deputy ministers and other aides sank in the St. Lawrence, luckily with nobody aboard. The Quebecers, looking ahead to their independence referendum, staged incredibly lavish receptions and parties to show their stuff as a sovereign state. At one bash for premiers and the media, enough food was left untouched to feed half the nearby town of La Malbaie.

Premier René Lévesque, meanwhile, was vastly amused by the growing dispute between two English-speaking provinces. At one point he joked privately, "Here I am, the separatist prime minister of Quebec, trying to keep peace between Ontario and Alberta."

Lougheed replied to Davis at a news conference packed with reporters from across the country. Explaining that Alberta had already provided a subsidy of $15 billion to the rest of Canada by selling oil for less than world prices, Lougheed steadfastly refused to negotiate revenue sharing. Davis's proposal was "completely unacceptable," he said, because it was "a clear attempt to change the basic concept and arrangements of Confederation which left the ownership of natural resources to the provinces." And the change, Lougheed added acidly, would apply only to a western resource, not to rich Ontario resources such as nickel, hydro power and forest products.

Most of the other premiers sided with Lougheed. Manitoba's Sterling Lyon, whose province had no oil to sell, called Davis's plan "just another move by those damned easterners." British Columbia's Bill Bennett insisted: "We won't let Ottawa do through taxation what it can't do through the Constitution." New Brunswick's Richard Hatfield was most caustic. "You just don't come up to a friend, shake his hand, and put the other hand in his pocket," said the Tory premier.

True to form, the *Toronto Star* applauded Premier Davis for a great "national" strategy (although the *Globe and Mail* bucked opinion in its major market and came down squarely for the western argument). The *Edmonton Journal*, just as predictably, chastized Ontario's familiar and self-serving appropriation of noble words such as "national" and "Confederation." In an editorial, the paper said:

> The "strain on Confederation" is a shibboleth invented by central Canadian politicians and businessmen to rationalize

> a simple grab for part of the West's prosperity. Obviously, there has to be some noble excuse for such a raid; it is transparent.... Today Ontario remains much wealthier than Alberta, in part because it has enjoyed major economic advantages under the National Economic Policy, which is 100 years old next month. In contrast, Alberta has enjoyed the full advantage of its energy resources for only six years.

Davis's plan came to nothing at the time, but within fourteen months the West would be subjected to a second and equally odious federal policy, the draconian National Energy Program.

It was December 13, 1979, and the federal Conservative government had just lost a confidence vote on its budget in the House of Commons. For the players in the energy dispute, everything changed instantly when the news spread across the country. Lougheed knew what it meant as soon as he heard about the government's defeat while attending a function at Edmonton's Royal Glenora Club. For the first and last time anybody can remember, Lougheed downed a few drinks too many in public, and nobody could blame him. The scent of Liberal victory was instantly in the air, and Lougheed realized that once again he would have to do battle with both Ontario and Ottawa.

The election on February 14, 1980, confirmed westerners' worst fears. The new majority Liberal government won only two seats west of Ontario, both in Winnipeg. But by increasing its support in Ontario from 32 seats to 52, and winning 74 ridings in Quebec, Trudeau's Liberals were within 10 seats of commanding an absolute majority in the two central provinces alone. Even today, westerners vividly recall their fury at seeing the Liberals win a majority long before election results began to trickle in from the western time zones. Although Joe Clark was hardly an effective prime minister, he was still a westerner and better attuned to western grievances than any national leader since John Diefenbaker. Clark had at at least mustered the courage to stand up to Ontario – but the result, as usual, was a centralist backlash that left westerners to fight on their own, without an ally in Ottawa.

For Davis and the Ontario government, this was a great luxury. Once again the premier was able to assume his favourite guise of national statesman and conciliator while Ottawa did the dirty work. But Davis, like many a leader who presumes to speak for colonials, never seemed to realize how obvious this was to many westerners, or how unpopular he became in the West. From then on, whenever he talked about the nation or the national interest, Davis was branded a hypocrite. The National Energy Program, when it came down in October 1980, was seen as Ontario's reward for helping to re-elect the Liberals. A year later, Lougheed convinced eight premiers at their annual meeting that they should demand changes to the NEP, and Davis was the only provincial leader to disagree. "Bill Davis killed any chance he might have had for the national [Tory] leadership that day," Lougheed says. The last traces of their friendship died too.

After Joe Clark called a federal leadership convention in 1983, Lougheed had his revenge when the Ontario premier began to make noises about running. Lougheed, who was in Washington when he heard about Davis's plans, immediately told his people to make his feelings clear. One of the authors, then a columnist with the *Edmonton Journal*, got a phone call from a top Lougheed aide: If Davis runs, the assistant said, Lougheed will do everything in his power to swing every single western Tory against him. When the resulting column appeared in the *Toronto Star*, Davis's people were furious. But their soundings were already telling them that the premier would face big problems in the West.

Davis soon did the prudent thing by announcing that he wouldn't run. He had been done in by qualities common to colonials the world over – long memories and a quick instinct for revenge.

The four years of federal Liberal rule after 1980 were exceptionally bitter and divisive for the whole country. Lougheed fought the Liberals with such devices as cutting oil production, but he also had to negotiate. His greatest fear, he now confides, was that Ottawa would take the province to court and win. This might have destroyed western authority over resources – a right that took twenty-five years to gain after Alberta and Saskatchewan entered Confederation in 1905. Alberta's legal case on pricing was "a 50-50 proposition," he felt, because of federal authority over interprovincial commerce and the leanings of the Supreme Court. Lougheed believes that because the Court is appointed by Ottawa, and six of the judges are from Central Canada, its decisions generally favour federal power. A court case might have allowed Ontario to turn its political victory on oil prices into a permanent legal one. (Alberta had already launched a challenge against the NEP's export tax on natural gas, and eventually won in the Supreme Court, but this case was much clearer. The province actually bought gas wells and exported the gas, then based its argument on the constitutional prohibition against one level of government taxing another.)

To avoid a defeat on pricing, Lougheed desperately needed to keep the political lines open. This was a tricky balancing act, since polls taken shortly after release of the NEP showed 23 per cent support for separatism in Alberta. But the negotiations continued, bouncing from Winnipeg to Ottawa and Montreal, until the premier signed an oil-pricing agreement with Trudeau in September 1981. This strange deal, which artificially projected price rises that never occurred, was far from ideal; in fact, many Albertans thought the premier had caved in. (A photograph of him drinking champagne with Trudeau after the deal was signed caused him more political harm than any other episode in his career.) But Lougheed believed the agreement was the best he could get. This was the first time in Canadian history, he argues, that a province had negotiated a change in a federal budget. Certainly the result was better than a legal or even military attack on the province's resources.

Such thoughts might seem paranoid today, but in 1980 many westerners accepted them as gospel truth. In this period, a taxi driver in Edmonton told one of the authors: "If the central government sends in the troops, I'll be the first one to blow up an oil well." Doug Christie, the WCC leader, drew huge crowds to rallies where he shouted "Free the West!" Rage was abroad, a true hatred for Trudeau and Marc Lalonde, the federal energy minister through much of the period. When Lalonde came to Alberta, the RCMP quietly laid on extra security because of death threats.

In 1982 the western economy was weakened by high interest rates and the cash drain imposed by the NEP. Much of Western Canada entered a profound slump, almost a mini-Depression, that hit bottom when oil prices crashed in 1986. Meanwhile, Southern Ontario began the most dramatic boom in its history, a climb that made Toronto a budding international powerhouse within six years. Much of this happened, westerners believe, because Ontario was in an ideal launch position after being subsidized throughout the oil boom. The Toronto area helped to snatch away western prosperity, and then accumulated wealth and development unprecedented in Canada.

Today's Liberal Ontario government seems very benign by contrast to the Davis regime; but then, it can afford to be. Western resource prices are hardly a threat. Ontario is clearly the economic engine of the nation, with a higher percentage of the Gross National Product in 1988 than it enjoyed in

1978 (41.3 per cent compared to 38.26 per cent; these figures show the dismal failure of so-called regional development). David Peterson, the Liberal premier, promises that if oil prices rise again, Ontario won't quarrel with paying the full price to the producing provinces – an easy pledge to make as long as reality doesn't intrude at $30 or $40 a barrel. "We've taken the view that in a deregulated business it's your resource, it's not our resource, and we have to take the consequences of that," the premier said in an interview. "We get the benefit if prices go down, and, in a cyclical economy, a resource-based economy like Alberta, then they're entitled to the benefit if they go up."

But it's revealing, too, that the parts of the free trade deal Peterson hates most are those that allow the producing provinces to sell their energy to the Americans. "We make a mistake just flogging this stuff across the border," he says. "We should be co-operating far more for the benefit of Canadians. I'm not talking about the price side, I'm talking about the supply side." The last remark is apparently meant to allay western concerns, but one nuance still raises suspicion; it's very hard to limit the market for a product without also limiting its price. Peterson seems unaware of the main reason westerners tend to seek markets in the United States rather than Ontario: Americans are always willing to pay the going rate, while Ontario often is not. Westerners would much prefer to sell to Canada, but only if the market isn't rigged.

Peterson points out that Ontario is buying Manitoba hydro and Alberta coal. In the case of coal, at least, the province could purchase for less in the United States. This is very nice, but it's a small return for all the years of western overpayment for Ontario finished products and energy subsidy for the industries that make them. Historically, Ontario seems interested in a truly national market only when it's allowed to buy cheap and sell dear. Peterson's government will have to sign a lot more western contracts before it erases that impression.

Lougheed cites one of the key reasons why western oilmen would rather do business with the United States. A whole generation of them trekked to Toronto in the 1950s and 1960s to get funding for their wells, but "they snubbed us, turned us down cold," recalls the former premier. "That's why the oil patch went to the States for funding." For this reason, southern Alberta has powerful links today with Texas, Oklahoma and other American oil centres. If these ties are dangerous to Canadian sovereignty, it's because the Ontario-based financial institutions refused the opportunity to do the job themselves. (This isn't Peterson's fault, of course. When reminded that westerners tend to hate the chartered banks, he replied, "So do I.") Many westerners believe that Ontario power brokers intentionally refused to help develop the resource, then tried to confiscate the profits after westerners went ahead in spite of them. It's little wonder the oilmen have no sympathy for the problems of Ontario industry, or that the NEP turned many of them into flat-out economic separatists. Within months after the program was implemented, some in the oil patch concluded that their only protection was to remove the oil industry as far as possible from the Canadian economic system. They had always been ardent advocates of free trade, but now they became almost fanatical. To the Canadian-owned companies in the oil industry, the best escape from meddling by Ontario and Ottawa was the right to sell energy freely to the United States. With the Conservatives' free trade deal they achieved much of what they wanted (although Ontario utilities and the National Energy Board are doing their best to dilute this right by searching for ways to limit natural gas exports).

Peterson has little taste for open hostility between Ontario and the West. He prefers to deal quietly with western leaders to get things done. "Have you noticed that neither Don Getty nor I employ the mean-spirited rhetoric of the past?" he asks. "We get on the phone, we try to solve problems. We put our energy ministers together, we compromise a little bit. There are two ways to fight. You can use any cheap comment you want and try to inflame passion, or you can fight as honourable people with a difference of opinion."

Getty and Peterson certainly get along better than Lougheed and Davis in their later days in office. Today's leaders also have a football connection – as a high school student in London, Ontario, Peterson watched Getty play quarterback for the University of Western Ontario Mustangs. "He was my hero," Peterson says. "He was big stuff when he was at Western. He doesn't take cheap shots. Some guys in this business, the first thing they do is take the cheap shot. But we try to work it out. Why? Because it's better for the country, that's why."

Peterson deplores the energy wars of the past, and he seems genuinely to care about the West's aspirations. But he also displays a powerful Ontario paternalism to which he seems completely oblivious. (Or perhaps he isn't; such attitudes never hurt an Ontario premier with his own voters.)

"This is a unique federation in the world," Peterson says, "in the sense that there's no other where one province is so big, relatively speaking you know, 41 per cent of the GNP, the most people, all that. My view is that Ontario wants to use that power constructively and positively. We're very strong federalists and very strong nationalists. We want to be as kind and sympathetic as possible to everybody else's problems. If Atlantic Canada has fish problems, we'd like to help, except that we can't." But Ontario is very friendly toward Quebec's goals, he argues, and is trying to help the West commercially with the coal and hydro deals.

This is the typical Ontario view: the province has the

power, will definitely keep it, and is obliged only to use it kindly, in a fatherly way, never to share it. As Peterson says in another context, "I'm not insensitive to the hinterland." It's amazing that he could even use the word, which the Oxford Dictionary describes, in part, as an area "of sparse population or inferior civilization."

Peterson also claims that "Ontario has probably the least sense of regionalism of any province in the country. Nobody says they're an Ontarian. They say they're Canadians." Westerners have a quick answer to this. Ontarians display as deeply rooted and obvious a sense of regionalism as anybody else in the country, but they are rarely conscious of this because federal policy has always suited their regional interests so well. Only in Ontario, therefore, do people assume that their regional goals are automatically "national" or "Canadian" goals. In every other province, and especially in Quebec and the West, people are used to feeling that their goals are in conflict with "national" ones. Outside Ontario, identification with the province is stronger for the simple reason that the province often represents the people better than the nation does. This is obvious in the labels people often use most proudly; Québécois, Albertan, British Columbian, Manitoban. In those provinces, words like "nationalist" and "federalist" are quickly spotted for what they often are – expressions of Ontario regionalism.

Even today, with free trade giving westerners more freedom to ignore Ontario when they sell resources and buy finished products, the same attitudes persist on both sides. The West still thinks like the colonial servants, and Ontario behaves like the imperial power. Our regional natures take a long time to change, especially when they have flourished for nearly 150 years.

Quite naturally, many westerners are deeply suspicious about promises of change. Ron Ghitter, a former Alberta Tory MLA who saw the system from the inside when he worked for the huge real estate company Trizec Corp. Ltd., doubts that the West has made any real gains. His company is a classic example of control from the centre. Although its headquarters are in Calgary, its primary owners are the Bronfman and Reichmann families (as equal shareholders). The company that controls Trizec, Carena Developments Ltd., has its offices in Toronto's Commerce Court. There is an illusion in Calgary that Trizec is a proud western company, but everyone on the inside knows where the big decisions are made – in Toronto.

"All the financial clout is still in the golden triangle of Ontario," says Ghitter. "I wish I weren't right. I wish this notion of the new western power were a reality. But because of my business experience I know how things really tick." Like many other westerners, he yearns for independence from Toronto's power. "Some day if I want to raise money I may not have to go to Toronto," he says. "Maybe I can go to San Francisco or Tokyo, and maybe I can do it by fax or phone. And we're better positioned for this because of free trade." But unlike Prime Minister Mulroney, who believes this trend is well advanced, Ghitter feels that nothing substantial will happen for many years. Ontario and Toronto simply set too much of the nation's business agenda to give up much control just because of one international deal.

Ghitter and others feel that Toronto, for all the anti–free trade sentiment there, may actually end up profiting most from the deal. All the major national companies based there – the retail giants, the developers, the banks – have built their regional networks across the country, Ghitter says. There's little more for them to exploit in Canada, so they're ready to expand beyond. "They've built their nests on our backs, and now they're ready to fly away."

Prime Minister Mulroney does a tricky balancing act when he talks about how free trade might alter the balance of power between Ontario and the West. On the one hand, he says Ontario doesn't have a right to all the country's industry, but, on the other, he argues that the province won't lose anything through the deal. Essentially, he says both that other regions can grow and prosper, and that Ontario can hold its dominant position. The logic of this is tough to spot, unless Mulroney means that all regions will begin to grow at Ontario's racehorse pace of the 1980s. So far, there's little sign of this.

"The great industrial heartland of Ontario will always be a powerful influence on Canada and . . . I'm happy about that," Mulroney said in an interview. "There's a great sophistication in the Ontario economy that pleases me a great deal. What didn't please me was the idea that other parts of the country could not have similarly sophisticated and well-developed economies – diversified economies....

"I didn't view the free trade agreement as anything of an instrument to repress any part of the country, but [as] an instrument that would liberate other parts of the country in the same way that Ontario went through an enormous expansion. Why not Ontario? Why not Atlantic Canada? Why not Alberta? And why not other parts of Canada?"

Yet Mulroney's ambitions for the West are limited. He does not believe the region needs its own financial institutions or should strive for them. Nor does he lament the astounding collapse of many western trust companies, commercial banks, mortgage companies and co-operatives – well over fifteen such failures since 1980 in Alberta alone. Although he takes no pleasure from losses incurred by many innocent investors (as well as by Ottawa's own Canadian Deposit Insurance Corporation), Mulroney believes that banking and finance should not be major industries for the West.

"Toronto's great strength is its world-class reputation in respect to the financial markets," he says. "It's developing into a real powerhouse.... And look at the head offices, the financial head offices that are located in Toronto.

"Now you see, I don't think that's necessarily bad at all. In fact, we can make a very strong case for all of us contributing to build a world-class financial institution centre in Toronto, provided that there are world-class centres of excellence that are being developed elsewhere."

Ottawa has put a great deal of money into agriculture and energy to make them "powerful centres of excellence where Western Canada and Alberta could be world-beaters in their own way. I don't think we can have it all. I don't think that each region of Canada has everything . . . Alberta and Quebec and Halifax, we can't all be New Yorks."

The instant and instinctive western reponse is that those western centres, if they are to grow and prosper, will often depend on money controlled in Toronto. And any westerner who has ever tried to buy a house or borrow money in hard times knows that the big chartered banks, based in Toronto and Montreal, are not always eager to lend. This is why the western provinces encouraged their own financial institutions in the first place – to give the region some freedom of choice, and to challenge the chartered banks with much-needed local competition. There remains a powerful feeling that these institutions failed partly because Ottawa and Central Canada sucked many billions out of the West through the National Energy Program. When this happened, land prices fell and the western groups were left holding worthless mortgages. Western collapse was inevitable, and many believe it was even welcome on Bay Street. Once again, the big banks were left almost unchallenged in the West.

Still, Mulroney seems to believe these grievances are becoming irrelevant, because in future the West will be supplied more and more by offshore capital. Computerization and deregulation of financial centres means that westerners will get their capital from Tokyo, San Francisco, or any of a dozen other centres, he argues. "This is why the deregulation of financial market [is] so important. If this happens, centres of excellence in the West will attract their own capital without going through other parts of Canada.... I can tell you that the Japanese for example were talking to me, and their focus is essentially on Western Canada . . . [and] they carry around enough money in their jeans on any given day to cause even me, carrying a large deficit, to open up my eyes." One proof of the claim is nearly $5 billion in Japanese investment in new western forestry projects.

The very thought of all this foreign investment, unregulated by Ottawa and out of Toronto's control, is enough to make Ontario nationalists blanch. With some reason, they fear a sell-out of resources and loss of sovereignty. This is the core of their growing feeling that Mulroney's policies will destroy the country. Western governments usually reply that the new enterprises are firmly regulated by provincial and federal law. Peter Lougheed goes a step further. He believes offshore capital should usually be a minority interest in a project, with Canadian investors always in control.

Whatever the solution, the banks can blame themselves for this great western hunger for foreign money. During the Depression, they shut one branch after another in western towns, evicted hundreds of families from farms, and built up a reservoir of hostility that persists today. Today the banks' behaviour is more discreet but no less brutal. Al Braden, former chairman of the Treasury Branches, says a chartered bank president told him in 1982: "We're giving up on the West. The economy is hopeless. With our problems in the West and Third World defaults, we have to pull back to Ontario and Quebec to be profitable." The banks were true to their word. With little thought of the profits taken from the region over many years, several recalled executives to the East and ordered western branches to curtail their lending. Few people in the West doubted that when the western institutions began to go down like bowling pins, Bay Street was quietly pleased. Western depositors, disappointed by the enduring fickleness of the banks, had been taking their business to these regional operations. When the western groups folded, God was back in his heaven and financial power was back in Toronto.

Generations of such experiences have taught westerners that the chartered banks are like rats: when times are good they feverishly sniff around to see what they can pick up, but at the first sign of trouble they scurry overboard. Ontario governments might have their own problems with the banks, but they watched this systematic discrimination against the West for years with little sympathy and even less concern for solutions. The banks have made it possible for westerners like Peter Aubry to say: "If I had the choice of buying the same car, same price, from Los Angeles or Oshawa, I'd take the one from L.A. They have a better understanding of the West down there.... It's easier to do business in the United States than in Canada."

Sometimes, Mulroney displays very similar reactions – fierce ones, in fact – especially when he takes on the anti-free trade forces in Ontario. Clearly he has no more tolerance for them than they have for him. "You see, the argument from those people in Toronto in the last election was that this trade with the Yankees was going to cost us [sovereignty]," he says mockingly. "But Ontario's exports rose dramatically in the last eighteen years to the United States.... The only thing that happened in Ontario, it became richer, not less sovereign. The *Toronto Star*'s selling more copies, the CBC's got a new twenty-four-hour service, there's a new building for the CBC....

"When you examine the Auto Pact, go back into the history of it, it was fought ferociously by a number of people – the New Democratic Party, the United Auto Workers . . . to name but two. Now they claim it as their own – they sired it, so intimate was their association with it! So I think they'll feel the same way about the free trade agreement, the critics of the free trade agreement, in twenty-five years."

Mulroney makes a clear distinction, however, between the people of Ontario and the groups that opposed free trade. "I campaigned on the free trade agreement," he says hotly, "with really quite strong opposition from the government of Ontario, the *Toronto Star*, most of the interest groups there, based in Toronto, and we finished the election with more seats in Ontario than any of our opponents . . . which is really quite remarkable when you consider the ferocity of the opposition."

Like many a Quebec politician before him, Mulroney betrays a visceral dislike of Ontario's power and influence. Often he sounds just like a westerner. It's hardly a coincidence that his election plank in 1988 – free trade – relied mainly on an alliance of the West and Quebec against Peterson and the nationalists. Without doubt, this is the national alignment that makes him feel most comfortable. If he can pick up a few seats in Ontario along the way, so much the better.

Mulroney certainly deplores the Ontario-centred federal policy that led to the National Energy Program. "I said then, in 1980 I think it was . . . that the National Energy Program is exactly like a hold-up at a gas station at three in the morning. That's what they did! No one with a brain in his head is placing in doubt the fact that the Liberal government went in and knowingly pillaged the economy of Alberta." To the Ontario-based nationalists, with their vision of a traditional Canada firmly in their power, Mulroney seems to be an emissary straight from hell. His attitudes and policies challenge everything they stand for – their assumption of right; their desire for quiet, submissive regions; their belief that only one view of Canada, their own, is legitimate.

Dave Barrett ran afoul of these people while he was a candidate for the NDP leadership in 1989. When he announced his candidacy, he dared to say that we shouldn't be obsessed with Quebec, because Canada has other problems too. Quebec may be a distinct society, he argued, but so is Alberta or British Columbia. He warned that Central Canada is so preoccupied with Quebec that it doesn't see the danger of western alienation.

At the height of the controversy, Barrett told the authors that "my biggest problem was with the Toronto-centred nationalists in my own party. These people think they own the New Democratic Party. Anybody who says anything they don't agree with is automatically a bumpkin." Or a bigot. During the leadership campaign, Barrett's NDP opponents stopped just short of calling him a redneck, but he refused to back down. "It's not a sin to worry about more than Ontario and Quebec," he said in Toronto. He knew he was representing a view that cut across party lines in the West and enjoyed a good deal of support among Ontario voters as well. But this didn't do him much good the night he lost the leadership to Audrey McLaughlin, largely because Ontario union leaders and other power brokers decided it was time to stop him.

One of the sorest points of all with westerners is Toronto's domination of the national media, which corresponds closely to Montreal's control of French CBC programming throughout the country. English-speaking westerners often find themselves watching hokey stereotyped images of their region. It's even worse for francophones, who are forced to watch and hear Quebec news masquerading as national news. There have been moves to change this, at least in English, through the CBC Newsworld channel's intense focus on all the regions (including Ontario). Anybody who cares to watch will quickly be filled to bursting with reports about pollution on the British Columbia coast, the latest doings of Winnipeg council, or fish plant closings in Atlantic Canada.

Newsworld is total immersion in regionalism, and a welcome addition to the programming on CTV, the regular CBC, or the Global network. Sometimes, this produces startling results: on election night in Quebec in 1989, one of the authors was the commentator for Newsworld's nationwide coverage – from a studio in Calgary. There's no reason that national analysis shouldn't come from anywhere in Canada, of course, but we are so used to seeing Toronto assume this role that the change seems peculiar.

Yet even Newsworld is still run from Toronto. Halifax and Calgary are the main production centres, but the managers there still have to consult the administrative unit in Toronto every day. Nobody in the operation doubts that Newsworld head Joan Donaldson is the boss, and she sits where English CBC bosses have always parked their posteriors, in Toronto. Others are trying to change this pattern, especially Izzy Asper, the Winnipeg media magnate and former leader of the Manitoba Liberal party. Late in 1989, Asper won control of the Toronto-based Global-TV network after a long wrangle with his former co-owners, Paul Morton and Seymour Epstein. He promised to produce more programming, especially drama, to reflect the West. And he infuriated many in the Toronto media when he said: "We are the orphans of Confederation and we resent it. Watch the irrelevance and the insignificance and colonialism with which Western Canada is portrayed on national television. We hope to make that different.... We regret that Toronto . . . really doesn't understand what 55 per cent of the land mass of Canada and 35 per cent of its population are all about. We don't feel the CBC and CTV have properly portrayed this country to its population and we feel that's one of our missions." A typical picture of westerners, he added, is "some farmer with a straw in his mouth standing by a tractor saying, 'Gosh the grasshoppers are bad this year.' "

Westerners know exactly what he means. Everyone who

keeps an eye on the national media sees the region routinely portrayed as a land of farms, drought, steers, trees, oil wells and rednecks. Seldom is there much focus on the growing urban vitality in such places as Vancouver and Winnipeg. But the Toronto reaction to Asper's remark, predictably, was cold fury. "What malarkey!" sneered Sid Adilman, a *Toronto Star* entertainment columnist. He chided Asper for failing to reflect the the West with the TV stations he already owned, and added: "That line plays well in Western Canada, but it's just an excuse for failure of risk-taking and putting money where the big mouth is."

A decade of astounding prosperity, it seems, has only reinforced Southern Ontario's notions about its superiority. In Toronto there's still a strong streak of puritanism that equates the city's wealth with virtue. If Toronto and Ontario are prospering, this reasoning goes, they must be right about everything, including the state of the nation. Westerners whine because they aren't smart or virtuous enough to be rich. Toronto was easier to bear when it was poorer, and even when it was more religious. Today the great metropolis sometimes seems to take its political and social thinking from Donald Trump.

Yet there is worry in Ontario that some small part of this massive influence might be chipped away. Thomas Courchene, a Queen's University academic, caught this mood perfectly in a 1988 paper called "What Does Ontario Want?"

> By the mid-1980s, Ontario was back in the *economic* driver's seat. Indeed, one would probably have to go back several decades to find a situation comparable to the mid-1980s dominant economic position of Ontario in the federation. However, the big difference is that, despite its tremendous economic clout, Ontario is no longer in the *political* driver's seat. This should surprise no one, given Ontario's recent initiatives. Moreover, both Meech Lake and free trade will ensure that Ontario will never regain the power that it was

once able to wield in the federation. And, as if to add insult to injury, the generally accepted perception of Mulroney's election strategy is to carve out a Quebec-West axis!

Courchene, a westerner, doesn't condemn this possibility; like any good academic, he merely observes it. But his point got considerable attention in the Ontario media, especially in the *Globe and Mail*. It seemed to raise a primal fear that Ontario might be plunging toward some lowly state of equality with the other provinces. The worries were groundless because free trade hardly seems to be killing Ontario. It allows westerners to buy and sell across the border, but Ontarians get exactly the same benefit. The Ontario conglomerates actually have an advantage because many are large enough to compete in the United States. In the West, there's a growing feeling that most regional companies do not yet have the maturity to thrive either in the States or against American competition in Canada. They might end up being sold to the Americans even while the big Ontario concerns grow richer. In the end, western business might trade Ontario domination for the doubtful joys of ownership in New York, Los Angeles or Dallas.

Even the goods and services tax, which is supposed to be the Tories' way of preparing the economy for free trade, carries a relative benefit to Ontario. It replaces the manufacturers' sales tax, which falls most heavily on Ontario because most industry is centred there. By lowering the rate and spreading the tax across the whole economy, Ontario will gain one more competitive advantage. What else is new?

By now, though, westerners are used to living with Ontario. They don't just sleep beside the American elephant, as Pierre Trudeau once suggested. There's another political pachyderm to the east that can do as much damage if it rolls over. The West is expected to feed it, water it and keep it contented. The trouble with this elephant is that it's hard to train, and often westerners can get its attention only by shouting at it or kicking it in the shin. It's a Canadian elephant and westerners are attached to it in a strange sort of way, but that doesn't necessarily mean they want to live with it forever.

SIX

Do Women Vote Up There?

MIDWAY THROUGH THE CAMPAIGN FOR ALBERTA'S Senate election in 1989, provincial Conservatives were alarmed. Nobody seemed interested in the oddest and most original election ever held in Canada – the vote to choose a nominee for a vacant Alberta Senate seat. The twenty people who turned up for one forum in Edmonton found themselves outnumbered by the seven candidates, their friends and assistants, and reporters. A later rally in Calgary drew only forty people and commentators began to predict a fiasco. The government's gamble that it could force Ottawa to accept the winner of the election began to seem foolhardy. If only 10 or 20 per cent of the voters turned out on October 16, Prime Minister Mulroney would simply laugh at the election, and so would the whole country. The blow to the prestige of Don Getty's Tory government and to the western drive for Senate reform would be catastrophic. Getty and his ministers, including Federal Affairs Minister Jim Horsman, began to sound desperate warnings about the dangers of a low turnout.

By any measure, the Senate election was a strange and unprecedented event. Albertans were being asked to vote in an election held under provincial law, for candidates of provincially registered parties, in order to change a federal institution. Yet federal parties were actually prohibited from putting up candidates, and MLAS and MPS were not allowed to run. Everyone knew there was no constitutional basis, and not much logic, to this vote. In fact the federal government for a time considered challenging the election in court, and might well have won. Nobody really believed the election would make Senate representation any more equal or effective, nor would it establish any legal precedent for regular elections. At best it would be an opinion poll to determine the province's favourite candidate for the Senate. The victor would be at the mercy of Prime Minister Mulroney, who still had the sole right to appoint senators. The election itself, grafted unnaturally to province-wide municipal elections, was a weird hybrid that seemed to puzzle the citizens.

The campaign was a surreal experience for the seven hardy souls, including four independents, who dared to run. For weeks they wandered the province, seeking vainly for signs of public interest. They were frustrated because there were no built-in events, no natural rallying points, no general election to excite the public. Two weeks into the month-long campaign they were exhausted from stumping their province-wide constituency. Stan Waters, the Reform Party candidate and a war veteran, said it was "like campaigning from Aberdeen to Naples." A longer campaign would "kill off all the candidates," he added. Disheartened, they blamed the media for the small crowds and urged people to get interested.

By all accounts the one man who wasn't worried was

Premier Getty. He believed that Alberta voters had a deep interest in Senate reform, and he thought they wanted to say so in an election. Getty staked a good deal of his flagging credibility on this conviction. He had called the vote against advice from party officials who argued that Albertans didn't care about the Senate as much as they let on. What if the voters don't show up on election day? the advisors asked. Worse, what if the Tory candidate is defeated?

But Getty forged ahead in his stubborn fashion, first by ordering the enabling bill into the legislature, then by picking an early election date. This was extremely dangerous for the Conservative candidate, Bert Brown, the West's most avid campaigner for a Triple E Senate. Just five months earlier the Tories had taken a kicking at the polls, at least by Alberta standards. They won only 59 of 83 seats and Getty lost his own Edmonton riding, an embarrassing outcome that forced him to run in a rural by-election. Now the anti-Tory mood was even stronger in the province. The Conservatives were heading for a twin disaster – a loss in the election and a humiliating lack of interest in the process itself.

By the last week of the campaign, the Tories knew their man would lose. The polls were devastating. The public ones showed Brown running far behind Waters and even Bill Code, the Liberal candidate. The Conservatives' private soundings were just as bad. But Getty gamely kept predicting a big turnout, and he was right about that at least. The results produced an astounding, powerful western call for Senate reform. A total of 641,519 people voted – only 200,000 fewer than had turned out for the previous provincial election. This amazed experts like David Ives, the province's deputy chief electoral officer, who had expected a turnout from 20 to 30 per cent, the traditional range for local elections. "It's a hell of a lot more than you'd see for just municipal voting," he said.

Waters and the Reform Party won by a huge margin with 259,292 votes, or 41.7 per cent of the ballots cast. Liberal Code polled 139,808 (22.5 per cent), while Brown, the Tory, trailed dismally with 127,638 (20.5 per cent). The election proved that Albertans were disgusted with Tories, both federal and provincial. But it also furnished Getty with the ammunition he needed to challenge the national system and demand the creation of a Triple E Senate. One of the great clarion calls of western alienation – the demand for a Senate that truly represents the provinces and regions – was sounded at Ottawa yet again.

Getty and many other Albertans now expected Mulroney to name Waters to the Senate in short order. Their logic seemed compelling: How could the prime minister deny the result of a democratic election? Wouldn't he just underscore the flaws of the Senate and his own damaging reputation for patronage politics? The outcome seemed so obvious that even some Ottawa mandarins and journalists expected Mulroney to move quickly. They were all wrong. For months Mulroney ignored Waters, then used him as a bargaining chip in the countdown to the deadline on the Meech Lake accord. Mulroney was offended by Getty's inconsistency; the premier had agreed in the 1987 accord to discuss Senate reform after Meech was ratified, then decided to hold a half-baked election. In doing so, Getty challenged the prime minister's right to name his friends to the juiciest pork barrel in the western world. This did not go down well in the prime minister's office, in the federal Tory party, or in the editorial offices of Ontario newspapers, including the *Toronto Star*. The mighty *Star*, generally thought of as liberal and friend of the little person, found itself defending both a Tory prime minister and the existing Senate. The election was "political grandstanding in an election year," an editorial said. At best it was "mischief, a silly attempt by Getty to pressure the federal government into Senate reform. At worst, it's a sham. Regardless of what happened . . . in Alberta, it's still Prime Minister Brian Mulroney's constitutional right to appoint whomever he wants – even cronies and hacks – to sit in the atrophied Upper Chamber of Parliament." The old Senate system, for all its ridiculous faults, was more resistant than Getty believed, partly because it suited the status quo in Ontario very well.

Getty and his advisors had made some crucial mistakes. They really expected, in their ardour for Senate reform, that a "snowball effect" would develop. Alberta's bold stroke would, they believed, create an irresistible national momentum for Senate election. This would quickly sweep aside the prime minister's objections and lead other provinces to hold similar votes. Soon the whole country would be clamouring to elect their senators. Other matters, such as equal representation from all provinces and the definition of powers, would fall into place almost magically. Behind Getty's initiative lurked some remarkably naive, romantic notions, and most of them came from his misreading of American history.

During the campaign, the premier liked to talk about the "Oregon example." He was referring to the first United States election for the Senate, held in 1904. Getty noted, correctly, that many western American states soon began to hold such votes, and by 1913 a constitutional amendment, the seventeenth, required all states to elect their senators. Until that time, the U.S. Constitution of 1787 had allowed state legislatures to select two senators each to send to Washington.

But the premier missed a crucial point. When the western states held their elections, they were not threatening the interests of the federal government or any other states. Each state had always had the absolute right to choose its own senators, and representation had always been equal (two senators from each state). The only dispute – a relatively small one – was over the method of selection. The American president couldn't say, as Brian Mulroney said of Alberta's election, "I'm not obliged to accept the result – the final choice is mine." In fact, the only resistance to the first American election came from those who were giving up the power of selection, the state legislatures. In 1904, the Oregon legislature rejected the result of the first vote. The state members refused to name the people's choice, a popular ex-governor, and substituted their own favourite. This brought another step in the speedy progress to Senate election – a bill that took all discretion away from the legislature. Mulroney today has the same power of refusal, but no province can remove it. The Canadian road to reform will be much longer and bumpier than the one the Americans travelled so long ago.

And yet, the need for reform seems so obvious to many westerners that they can hardly believe others don't see it. The region's opinion of the appointed chamber has changed little since Bob Edwards wrote in 1920: "When a man quits turning around to look at a pretty girl he is old enough, almost, for the Senate." From the time of Confederation, the body was meant to be a chamber of "sober second thought" more than a forum for regional representation. The American Civil War frightened any thoughts of regional equality out of the Fathers of Confederation. They were appalled by the spectacle of states so strong that they could actually make war on the federal government, and they observed that a key feature of American federalism was equal representation in the Senate.

During the Confederation debates, only Prince Edward Island proposed an equal number of senators for each colony. The idea of election was dismissed out of hand because the real function of the Upper Chamber was to act as a check on popular democracy. George-Etienne Cartier intoned: "There must be a power of resistance to oppose the democratic element" (a natural enough sentiment for a wealthy railroad promoter; Cartier's greater sin was to secure Ottawa as the national capital). The journalist Thomas D'Arcy McGee made the point even more clearly: "We run the risk of being swallowed up by the spirit of universal democracy that prevails in the United States.... The proposed Confederation will enable us to bear up shoulder to shoulder to resist the spread of this universal democracy doctrine." Thus Canada ended up with a Senate that had a rough regional balance (this much was essential to coax the Maritime provinces into Confederation), but no provision for election or equality among provinces. At Confederation, Ontario had 24 senators; Quebec, 24; and the Maritimes, 24. As the country expanded, the regional principle continued to apply: the western provinces were allowed six senators each, Newfoundland got six when it entered in 1949, and the Yukon and Northwest Territories were at last granted one each in 1975. This rounded out the current total of 104 Senate seats.

The main problem with the Senate has been evident for at least one hundred years. Ontario and Quebec, the provinces with the most people and therefore the most seats in the House of Commons, had the strongest regional representation. The smaller provinces, with fewer MPs, had to settle for the weaker regional voices as well. The entire system was, and is, based on the weight of population. In this sense, Canada isn't a true democratic federation at all. It is, in fact, the only one in the western world that does not in some way recognize equality of states or provinces in a body of the central government. The only small comfort is that the Senate, not being elected, doesn't have the authority to exercise the massive powers available to it in theory. If it did, the smaller provinces might feel even more oppressed than they do now. Getty's quixotic election was in one way a dangerous gesture. An elected Senate based on inequality could wreck the country, as Prime Minister Mulroney has often warned.

Yet Canadians have little appreciation of how peculiar the country is. Cecil Edwards, official historian of the Oregon state legislature, was amazed to learn that the Canadian Senate isn't elected. "You're pretty despotic," he said. "Your system seems a relic of the monarchy, and it's a restriction of the suffrage vote." He paused and added, quite seriously, "Do women vote up there?" Edwards is clearly no expert on Canada, but he's correct about the archaic nature of the Senate.

As other federations "nationalize" and feel a tighter sense of identity, we "provincialize," or pull farther apart. This happens even though our central government has tremendous power, both in theory as well as in practice. Taxation, control over interprovincial commerce, the War Measures Act – all these devices, and many more give Ottawa far more theoretical control over this country than Washington has over the United States. The U.S. Constitution provides the federal government with only those powers that are set down in the constitution. All the rest go to the states. In Canada, it's the other way around – the federal government has these important "residual" powers, which give it a tremendous advantage as the country changes and the government assumes new duties.

And yet, from Hawaii to Alaska to Florida, Americans undoubtedly feel a much more compelling sense of nationhood and pride than Canadians do. So do Australians and West Germans. In all those countries, people believe the national system is basically fair, so they trust the central government to play a proper, evenhanded role. And they feel that way largely because in one legislative chamber, the states or provinces are fundamentally equal. Canada has a great deal to learn from all of them.

In Ottawa and Ontario, it is often claimed that a Triple E Senate and the British parliamentary system can never coexist. Australia proves the folly of this argument. Since the Commonwealth of Australia was formed as a self-governing federation on January 1, 1901, the Australian states (now six) have elected an equal number of members to the Senate. Australia's founding fathers, a wiser and more fair-minded crowd than their Canadian counterparts, created a body modelled closely on the American Senate. "This was considered the price, which had to be paid, to attract the smaller colonies into the federation," according to *Strengthening Canada*, the Alberta legislature's 1985 report on Senate reform. "It was a unique institution in the sense that it was an elected upper chamber quite unlike any similar House in the British Empire."

The Australians also had a much stronger notion of how to make their new constitution legitimate; it was written largely by people elected only for that purpose, and then submitted twice to the voters for ratification. As Alexander Brady explained in his classic 1947 text, *Democracy in the Dominions*: "It was freely and vigorously debated on hundreds of platforms throughout the continent, and was submitted to the electors for approval. On its first submission to the citizens of New South Wales it failed to obtain the required number of votes. Further amended to meet the criticisms of labour and to conform more fully with democratic logic, the projected union was duly accepted in New South Wales and the other colonies." Canada's Constitution, written by colonial leaders and never subjected to popular approval, seems puny and undemocratic by contrast. The modern equivalent – eleven leaders meeting mostly in private – is no better.

Today the Australian Constitution can be amended only through a referendum that wins a national majority, as well as a majority in four of six states. Australians would never dream of allowing the prime minister and the state leaders to change the nature of their country at a private meeting, as Canada's leaders tried to do with Meech Lake. The fundamental law of the country is too important to be left to politicians. Because the nation was born in democracy, few Australians question the basic legitimacy and fairness of their country. Canadians, especially westerners, do this every day, in large part because they have never had a direct voice in nation-building.

It's tempting to suggest that we need to begin all over, with an assembly chosen from all parts of the country to write a constitution that fairly represents everyone, including the West and Quebec. The collapse of the Meech accord makes this even more imperative. The Americans did this two centuries ago, the Australians at the turn of this century, but the idea is still a bit forward and radical for colonial Canada. This might sound naive to Central Canadians who see Ontario's power and Quebec's special interests as obstacles that can't possibly be overcome. They're welcome to hold these views, but they should know that westerners are intimately familiar with all the problems. Westerners do not stop looking for remedies to inequality just because their ideas are dismissed as naive by people with a powerful interest in the status quo. Many westerners came to Canada in the first place because they wanted to escape bad governments and find equality. As long as the region stays in Canada, dismissals from Central Canada won't stop them from trying.

Australia's Senate is far from perfect, largely because it has often been dominated by national parties and their demand for party discipline. Because of this, Brady noted, "the thinly peopled states have been disappointed because the Senate has not become their aggressive defender." The situation improved in the 1960s with the introduction of proportional representation, a measure that gave more influence to small parties. Party discipline has also weakened slightly, but senators still tend to forget regional causes in their rush for promotion. One of the great flaws in the Australian system is that senators can be promoted to cabinet (as they can in Canada). American senators don't face such temptation, and this is a major reason why they almost always vote their state interests rather than the party line.

Despite these problems, though, the Australian Senate is a far more effective defender of regional interests than is its Canadian cousin. At the very least, as the Alberta Senate report explained, Australian senators from less populous states "have played an important role in representing state interests within their party." Canadian senators are more likely to spend their time defending the party's interests and polishing its machinery in their provinces. Senators from Western Canada have never been accused of acting like fierce defenders of their provinces or the people. The average citizen would never dream of going to these people to get a problem solved in Ottawa.

Westerners with a grievance against the federal government are forced to fight their battles through the premiers and provincial legislatures. In a country as diverse as Canada, with no outlet at the centre for regional grievance, local chieftains are a necessary force. Political scientist Roger Gibbons cites the shortcomings of the Canadian system compared to the American one in his book on regionalism in Canada and the United States: "Premiers enjoy a near monopolistic position with respect to territorial representation in the national political arena. They are able to capitalize on territorial conflict to their own electoral advantage at home.... State governors, facing tough competition from U.S. senators and congressmen, are less able to exploit territorial conflict to their own political advantage, and are thus less likely to fan the coals of territorial conflict."

The best way to spike the regional power of the premiers is to divert a large part of it into a Triple E Senate – and that, curiously enough, would make Ottawa even more important in the nation's life than it is today. Few people seem to realize that the West's Triple E crusaders are actually offering a great boost to the democratic authority of central government. But that authority would at last reflect the wishes of the whole country, not just of the two big provinces.

Where Quebec's unique character needs protection, this could be done through a series of double majorities and vetoes in matters of language and culture. A majority of French-speaking senators, as well as a majority of the whole Senate, would have to approve such bills. In some cases, francophone senators could kill a measure endorsed by a majority. All the best studies on Senate reform propose such solutions to Quebec's very reasonable objections. Quebec would enjoy more control than it has now, and the smaller provinces would at last gain a measure of regional equality.

Using the Americans as a model for anything Canadian is a dangerous business, especially in Ontario, with its ancient Loyalist sentiment. Westerners are less offended. Our cross-border ties are stronger in commerce, culture and kinship. From 1898 to 1914, half a million American immigrants moved to the West. They were welcomed by nearly everyone, including politicians, businessmen and journalists. By 1911, 21 per cent of Alberta's population was American born. As Howard Palmer writes in *Strangers and Stereotypes*: "Government officials regarded these settlers as ideal since they brought farm skills, capital and machinery which would enable them to farm successfully in Western Canada. The province's opinion leaders . . . also realized that the Americans could help them establish common schools, churches, community, and political institutions which they both regarded as essential to 'civilized' life." There was little prejudice against Americans then and there is little today. Westerners don't want to be Americans, but they have never seen much threat in American models for commerce or government. Indeed, the Triple E reformers believe Canada would be stronger, more united, and better able to resist American encroachment if it adopted some American methods. And the most appealing model of all is the American Senate.

Without question, the United States Senate works efficiently as a forum for making all states feel that they have a strong voice in the Union. Alaska, with a half-million people, has two senators, the same number as California, with nearly thirty million. Rhode Island and Delaware are as well represented as New York. This doesn't bother Americans in the slightest because they know that the larger states have far more members in the House of Representatives. (Canadians who reject the Triple E notion often forget that Ontario and Quebec would still dominate the House of Commons.) The Alberta report on the Senate says: "The 25 smallest states in the Union, although they contain less than 20 per cent of the nation's total population, hold 50 per cent of the seats in the Senate. This numerical imbalance between the number of seats and the population of a state has never become a significant political problem. The notion of equal representation of the states is a well-entrenched principle of the American political system."

Senators have far more status and power than members of the Lower House, a situation impossible to imagine under the current system in Canada. Often the senators have personal staffs of eighty to ninety people. This might seem extravagant; a Canadian senator with a staff so large would need a recreation director to keep them busy. But American senators sit on many committees and must deal with every national issue as well as all their local ones. There are only one hundred of them, but they generate their own legislation, examine bills from the House, and confirm many presidential appointments, including those to the Supreme Court. They ratify international treaties and try officials impeached by the House (this threat chased Richard Nixon from office). Many have more power and prestige than the governors of their own states – a fact that helps explain why so few Canadian premiers are really hot for an American-style Senate. Senators from relatively small states can become remarkably influential if they have the skill and ambition. The late Henry ("Scoop") Jackson, from Washington State, and Mike Mansfield, of Montana, became international figures as well-known as many members of presidential cabinets.

But all senators, no matter how famous or powerful, depend completely on the voters in their home state, and they ignore those electors at their peril. A senator who fails to block a bill that hurts the state, or neglects a benefit that might have been snatched, can be unemployed in a hurry. Often a half-dozen equally ambitious people, from state legislators to the governor, are panting to take the senator's place. It's little wonder that the senators and state Representatives, too, become adept at spotting and grabbing advantage. This explains why federally supported industry is spread so widely across the United States. David Kilgour, the Edmonton Southeast Tory MP who was expelled from the caucus, relates an amazing fact: components of the CF-18 jet fighter are manufactured in 42 of the 50 states. When the decision on maintenance contracts for the same aircraft was made by the Canadian cabinet, almost all the work went to Montreal, even though Winnipeg submitted a superior bid. Kilgour adds, in a draft chapter for a new book on Canadian federalism: "Similarly, Washington's mammoth super-collider project was awarded to a community in rural Texas. Which Canadian anywhere today believes that the Mulroney government would award a project of comparable importance to a location outside the Toronto-Ottawa-Montreal triangle?"

This sort of thing happens in the United States because senators have real power, not just to take action themselves, but to influence the president. They use it to horse-trade shamelessly for the benefit of their own states, often in the crassest way possible. The smaller Canadian provinces, with no such champions, are reduced to blustering or begging, often in impotent rage. Politically, Canada has become a welfare state where the small provinces depend on federal generosity.

Combine this with the most rigid party discipline of any western democracy, and we have the fine mess of modern Canada. This discipline prevents even elected MPS from acting in their own regional interests. Two striking examples were the rush by Tory MPS from all regions to support the goods and services tax, and the initial all-party chorus of support for Meech Lake in 1987. The first display resulted from iron-fisted party discipline within the government party; the second came from the slavish desire of all parties to curry favour in Quebec. In both cases, cries of rage from voters were ignored or simply overriden. Ironically, it was left to the Senate – the pathetic, decrepit, unelected Senate – to register small gestures of support for the voters. Kilgour says: "Canadian voting practice allows all three party leaders to have their followers vote as robots virtually always." With a few exceptions, MPS dread being denied promotion and the prime minister's smiles. As they all know very well, there is no parliamentary life in Ottawa outside the party caucuses.

Behind this rigid discipline, with its poisonous effect on regional needs, lies another absurd Canadian tradition. The government can consider itself defeated if it loses even the smallest vote in the Commons. In Britain and most other

Commonwealth countries, defeat ensues only if the government loses a vote on a major bill. A Canadian prime minister, though, can call an election on the most frivolous grounds, even, for example, if the government loses a motion to adjourn the House. In these circumstances party discipline becomes extremely important. As Kilgour says: "The Whips of government parties have for decades used the possibility of an early election to brow-beat all but the most independent of their members into voting the party line on virtually every issue which arises." Because the party line will often be determined by the interests of Ontario and Quebec, which have the most MPs, the smaller provinces again lose their voice.

At the very least, Canada needs a change of rules in Parliament to specify that the government can be defeated only on major bills. Another big step would be a statement, like the one in the West German Constitution, that elected officials shall not be "bound by orders and instructions and shall be subject only to their conscience." Anything that weakened party discipline would help MPs from small provinces fight for their voters' interests.

Again, the American system represents regional interests much more effectively. Senators and Representatives routinely cross party lines to vote their regional interests. Other members rarely hold this against them because a lost vote never means an election and perhaps a lost job. In both Houses, Republicans and Democrats combine in territorial voting blocs to garner favours for a whole region – the Mountain states, the Sun Belt or New England. Strategies like this helped win much of the defence industry for the South. Committees of Congress supervise departments of the executive branch, and members force everything from budget cuts to more service for their states. Canadian parliamentary committees are puny things by comparison; dominated by party whips, they produce plenty of partisan wind but few results. Kilgour found that, since 1969, only one item, for $10,000, was ever deleted by parliamentary committees that examine government budgets. And by the time that was done, the money had already been spent.

All the checks, balances and regional protection built into the American system make it virtually impossible for any state to suffer the fate of Alberta. According to a study for the C.D. Howe Institute, Alberta between 1961 and 1985 paid $100 billion more into the federal treasury than it received. The primary cause of this amazing drain on Alberta's economy was energy prices that were kept artificially low by federal policy. In 1981, after the National Energy Program kicked in, the outflow was an astounding $7,960 for every man, woman and child in Alberta. This simple fact explains why Albertans tend to be so fierce in their demands both for fair policies and for structural reform. The annual per-capita contribution made by Albertans from 1961 to 1985 was $1,956. In the same twenty-five-year period, Ontario and British Columbia, the only other provinces to run a net deficit, paid $17.7 billion and $3.78 billion, respectively. This works out to $132 per capita in B.C. and $126 in Ontario, paltry sums compared to Alberta's astounding contribution. All other provinces received far more than they gave: Quebec, for instance, got a net benefit of $91.4 billion ($562 per capita); Newfoundland got $28.3 billion ($2,054); and Nova Scotia $54 billion ($2,626). Alberta has made a contribution unequalled by any other province in Confederation. And the province made it with a resource that can never be renewed.

This study is not wacko western economics. Prepared mainly by two distinguished economists, Mike Percy at the University of Alberta and Robert Mansell at the University of Calgary, it was to be published jointly by the C.D. Howe Institute and the University of Alberta's Western Centre for Economic Research. Because the conclusions are far from the standard fare of Toronto think-tanks, the C.D. Howe Institute was understandably jittery and put the study through careful examination. Two independent reviews found the numbers and methodology to be solid. C.D. Howe decided to publish even though, as one observer said, "They know where their bread is buttered and it's not in Alberta."

Percy and Mansell also conclude that the NEP was the crucial factor that kicked Alberta into deep recession in 1982, primarily because it pulled out money and killed investment at the same time. Oil and gas activity declined disastrously, while Texas and Oklahoma, which faced similar economic problems, continued to do fairly well. Although the resulting Alberta recession was very damaging, it would have been even deeper if the provincial goverment had not stepped in with huge programs for oil and other industries affected. Largely as a result, the total provincial debt tops $8 billion. Ottawa created the recession, the province cushioned it, and now Albertans have to pay. Many of them feel today that only an elected Senate with real authority could have blocked the NEP, or at least altered it to a less damaging form. More than any other Canadians, Albertans know that Ottawa's goodwill is a fragile flower, and they find that it blooms most readily when oil prices are low. At other times the only defence is built-in political power that can't be subverted by the economic fears of Central Canada. The best guarantee would be a Triple E Senate with a temporary suspensive veto over House legislation.

Only a decade ago, anyone who advanced the idea of an elected Senate was considered a crank by most federal politicians and bureaucrats, and nearly everyone east of Kenora. This attitude, entrenched since Confederation, prevented all but the tiniest reforms to the Senate, and sometimes even those had to be forced on the country. In 1930 the first woman senator, Mrs. Cairine Wilson, was named by Prime

Minister Mackenzie King. He was able to do this only because, the year before, the British Privy Council had overturned a Canadian Supreme Court ruling that declared that women were not "persons," and therefore could not be senators. The appeal to Britain was initiated by five Alberta women, a well-known fact that shows how long the urge to constitutional reform has simmered in that province. Social reality again intruded in 1965, when the Constitution was amended to require that senators named after that date retire at age seventy-five. In 1969, a setback occurred when the position of government leader in the Senate was enacted. This leader serves in cabinet at the prime minister's pleasure, and his or her main job is to enforce the will of the House on the Senate. Nothing could be further from the notion of regional representation. In 1975, the Yukon and Northwest Territories at last got their Senate seats (which had been eliminated when Alberta and Saskatchewan became provinces in 1905).

None of this tinkering changed the fundamental irrelevance of the western world's most useless legislative chamber. But things suddenly began to happen in 1978, and the man behind the first formal proposal for real Senate reform was, oddly enough, Pierre Trudeau. He had decided that something must be done for the West.

One night in 1975, after another of his dismal visits to hostile western territory, the prime minister was in a thoughtful mood as he was being driven to the airport. His Liberal party had done better than usual in the West the year before; it had won 15 western seats in the general election, compared to only seven in 1972. But the Liberals held only one-quarter of the 60 ridings in the entire West and North, and none at all in Alberta, the Yukon or the Northwest Territories. After an initial burst of Trudeaumania in 1968, when the Liberals won 28 western and northern ridings, the usual malaise had set in. Westerners mistrusted the federal government in general, and they were developing a lively dislike of Trudeau in particular. In a few years these attitudes would harden into a poisonous hatred that startled the whole nation. For the moment, though, Trudeau wondered what he might do to make westerners more contented with the country and his government. He posed the question to Nick Taylor, then the Alberta Liberal leader, who was sitting beside him in the back seat of the car.

"One thing you could try is electing the Senate," replied Taylor, whose provincial party had never won an Alberta seat under his leadership, and wouldn't until 1986. Taylor made the point that westerners want most to be treated as equals, to feel they have lasting power that doesn't depend strictly on the goodwill of any government. He recalls that Trudeau thought about this for a moment and replied: "What if half the senators are elected and I appoint half?"

Great idea, Taylor said at once. He believed that if Trudeau actually did this, the pressure to elect all senators would be irresistible within twenty years.

The prime minister promised to consider their talk when he got back to Ottawa. Taylor wasn't encouraged, though, when Trudeau told him on the phone six weeks later that "some of the guys" didn't like the idea.

What guys? Taylor asked.

The westerners here in my office, Trudeau said. This didn't surprise Taylor; he realized that western Liberals close to Trudeau didn't care to share their precious influence with anything so potentially powerful as an elected Senate. One of them later told Taylor that westerners would be happy when they got "on the gravy train with everybody else."

The election idea was forgotten in a hurry, but the notion of Senate reform stuck with Trudeau. Actually, it wasn't as alien to Liberal thinking as the public believed at the time.

In the early 1970s, Izzy Asper, then the leader of the Manitoba provincial Liberals, had convinced the federal party to pass a resolution favouring a Triple E Senate (although the term wasn't used then). Asper accomplished this, he says, "by telling them that I wouldn't leave the hall as a Liberal if they didn't accept it." Asper then had the familiar experience of seeing a western resolution virtually ignored by the government for years. More than a decade later, Asper parted company with John Turner when the Liberal leader refused to embrace the Triple E cause.

When Trudeau's proposal came in 1978, it bore no similarity to Asper's grand design for equality. The government produced Bill C-60, a strange mixture that clearly showed all the contradictory pressures on a reform-minded prime minister. The Senate would be renamed the House of the Federation; there would be 118 members, 59 of whom would be appointed by the House of Commons, 57 by the provincial legislatures, and two by the federal cabinet to represent the Yukon and Northwest Territories. To handle tricky language legislation, a majority of both French- and English-speaking members would be required. Across the country there was an instant uproar. Instead of putting an end to patronage, the critics said, Bill C-60 would merely spread it to the provinces. The clumsy new chamber would be handcuffed by party factions controlled straight from provincial capitals. The government submitted the bill to the Supreme Court for review, and the judges, in a sensible mood, quickly declared it beyond the power of Parliament to enact. Lost in all the fuss was a real nugget of federal generosity. By offering to give the right to make federal Senate appointments to the Commons, the prime minister was relaxing his personal hold on patronage – at least in theory. (A strong prime minister in a majority Parliament would still be able to stuff his favourites into federal seats in the reformed pork barrel.)

Trudeau's proposal owed nothing to Australia, and it certainly wasn't American. More than anything else, it was German, a fascinating point little noted at the time. The West German Bundesrat has been around in one form or another since 1815, and the modern version is appointed entirely by the governments of the states, or Laender. Usually the Laender nominate their state premiers and other ministers. The whole gang from each state must vote *en bloc* according to the precise instructions of the government back home. Trudeau, who often regarded the provinces with outright contempt, was about to give Canadian premiers some of the same power. This would surely have made for some monumental federal-provincial battles on the old Senate floor.

The German Bundesrat actually works very well, even though it isn't elected or equal in representation (states with the most people get the most seats). But it serves as a kind of permanent federal-provincial conference with authority to review federal laws. One of the best features is that state bureaucrats, who enforce these federal laws, identify problems in committee hearings before the bills are passed. That point alone would solve many problems and save many millions of dollars in Canada. But the reaction after 1978 showed how alien the idea of provincial appointment is to most Canadians. As the Senate-Commons committee on Senate reform noted in 1984, the system is essential for Germany because the states administer federal laws. In Canada, with its much stronger provinces, Parliament could end up taking orders straight from premiers, and this would produce "a hybrid amounting to a monstrosity." A Teutonic monstrosity at that.

The Senate was virtually ignored in the momentous constitutional debate of 1980 and 1981, largely because it seemed minor compared to the complex problem of finding agreement on patriation and a Charter of Rights and Freedoms. The only change to the Senate's role was a veto limit of 180 days for constitutional changes. But the reform issue still had momentum, and once again, some of it was provided by Trudeau. In December 1982, the Liberal majorities in both Houses struck a committee to study how the Senate could be reformed "to enhance the authority of Parliament to speak and act on behalf of all Canadians in all parts of the country." Two years later, after reviewing twenty years of proposals and holding hearings across the country, the committee concluded "that the Canadian Senate should be elected directly from the people of Canada. An appointed Senate no longer meets the needs of the Canadian federation. An elected Senate is the only kind of Senate that can adequately fill what we think should be its principal role – the role of regional representation."

For the first time, the senators themselves agreed to put their jobs at risk in an election. This was no small step, and many westerners drooled at the prospect. But the committee members couldn't force themselves to go the whole way to a true Triple E Senate. The report said: "Equal representation in the Senate would tilt the balance too far and would be unacceptable to the vast majority of Canadians, not only to those living in the two largest provinces." The committee members' authority for this last statement was doubtful, but on it they based their whole proposal. Ontario and Quebec would keep their 24 seats each, but representation from the West would be doubled, to 48 seats from the four provinces (the equal of the central provinces). Atlantic representation would increase from 30 to 42 senators. Once again, there was to be no recognition of provincial equality in the regional body. Ontario and Quebec would still have the advantage, although a smaller one.

But the Senate, being elected, would have real authority, and this made the proposal extremely threatening to the smaller provinces. Unless they showed absolute regional solidarity on crucial issues, they could still be overwhelmed by central provinces in a dangerous Double E Senate (elected, effective, but still unequal). The National Energy Program could have passed this Senate as easily as it breezed through the unreformed Upper Chamber. Before the Trudeau government could take action (if any were ever intended), the Liberals were defeated by Brian Mulroney's Tories in the 1984 election. And the last thing the Conservatives wanted was an elected Senate to take the shine from their gigantic nationwide majority. Like all new Canadian governments, the Tories thought they could still every whisper of regional discontent just by exercising their talents. "National reconciliation" was Mulroney's goal, and he meant to achieve it without any help from the Senate, a body whose Liberal majority he despises to this day.

Zeal for reform continued to grow in much of the West, however, and especially in Alberta. The pressure was so intense that the Lougheed government formed a committee on November 23, 1983, to study the Senate question, even though the premier himself wasn't keen on the idea. Lougheed had always felt, and still does, that the goal was worthy but so difficult to achieve that all the energy was virtually wasted. As one of the strongest leaders in western history, he believed that premiers could be the true elected senators if they stayed united. But the Alberta committee, once turned loose on the subject, ran off in another direction. Its 1985 report called for true Triple E representation in a vastly reformed Senate. There would be six senators from each province and two from each territory, for a total of 64, all elected at large in their jurisdictions. They would be able to initiate any legislation but money bills, have the power to amend all House legislation and veto anything but a supply bill (although the House would be able to override any amendment or veto). Language issues would be subject to a double majority of French- and English-speaking senators. The Senate would also be empowered to ratify non-military treaties. And it would be kept out of the prime minister's clutches by abolishing the position of government leader, and by making senators ineligible for cabinet posts. This Senate would be more effective than the flawed Australian version, but far less imposing than the all-powerful American model (it would lack, for instance, the authority to review Supreme Court appointments). A more typical Canadian compromise is difficult to imagine.

When Don Getty took over from Lougheed in late 1985, he quickly became a true believer, a zealot for Senate reform. Liberal MLA Nick Taylor had actually been the first to suggest a Senate election, but Getty surprised everyone by taking him up on it. The premier also spent a good deal of his time lobbying other western premiers who hadn't yet seen the light. Eventually they all came aboard, but with varying degrees of enthusiasm and dedication. Often it seemed they were just trying to keep Getty happy with fine statements of principle that didn't cost them much. In British Columbia, Bill Vander Zalm at first seemed reluctant to abandon the traditional coastal view that his province should be considered a region equal to the Prairies, Ontario, Quebec and Atlantic Canada. He came aboard in 1987, however, and his eagerness for reform now seems to rival Getty's. Manitoba and Saskatchewan fell into line at the annual western premiers' conference in Parksville, British Columbia, in May 1988. (Something about the sea air, inhaled while the premiers met in private session on a yacht donated for the occasion by a millionaire, did wonders for western solidarity.) Saskatchewan's Grant Devine now feels that something must be done and the Triple E model is as good as any, although he isn't very passionate about it. After the Alberta Senate election, Manitoba's Gary Filmon promised to consider an election for a Senate vacancy that comes up in late 1990. He became the West's most ardent advocate of Senate reform during the Meech Lake debate, yet the only real change, after more than twelve years of study and discussion, is that a westerner who shouts "Senate reform" on an Ottawa street will not necessarily be run out of town.

In the spring of 1990, there were 353 assorted journalists in Ottawa's Parliamentary Press Gallery, and many of them laboured under an odd delusion. They thought the sun rose over the Château Laurier and set behind the Supreme Court building. Most of them couldn't help it; the pace of life on Parliament Hill is so frantic, the scrums and news conferences so abundant, the demands of editors so compelling, that they barely have time to eat and sleep, let alone ponder the rest of the country. The radio and TV reporters and crews are like galley slaves pulling the oars to a mad drummer's beat. Just to keep up is to survive. Pack journalism on the Hill, a growing problem for fifteen years, has become a menace to life and limb. The scrums (Pierre Trudeau once called them "scums") are seething masses of microphones, cameras, curses and elbows. Every day the Government and Opposition pump out reams of reports, analyses, assessments, minutes and other documents. No reporter has time to read a fraction of them (although the best, like *Ottawa Citizen* columnist Marjorie Nichols, make time to study the most important). A few Ottawa journalists have a fairly good idea of what really happens almost every day; a few more have a fair idea most days; the majority are just trying to get through the days without being trampled by the competition. The best equipment for survival on the Hill is no longer a brain, it's a long arm with a tape recorder at the end.

None of this is very conducive to the understanding of "regional" issues. The best reporters from outside the Golden

Triangle soon discover that few know what they're writing about. If their story doesn't appear in Ottawa right away, it sinks to the bottom of a deep pit, even if it has a significant "national" twist. Geoff White, the *Calgary Herald*'s fine Ottawa correspondent for five years, explains: "What you write has more impact if it's seen immediately in the capital area. The *Globe and Mail*, the *Toronto Star*, the Montreal *Gazette*, the *Ottawa Citizen*, *Le Devoir* – those are the ones that people see the same day. When the regional newspapers show up the issue has long passed."

White once wrote a story revealing that West Edmonton Mall received the only regional expansion grant given to Alberta for an entire year. This was fairly big news in the province; both the *Herald* and the *Edmonton Journal* carried it. But nothing happened in Ottawa until many months later, when the auditor general criticized the grant in his annual report. Suddenly everyone was interested, the national wires hummed with the "news," and White had the strange experience of chasing his own story all over again. "A lot of the time many regional issues get glossed over," he says. "An outstanding example is the way energy has been covered over the past five years. Once it slipped off the agenda of Central Canada, it slipped off the national agenda. But there were still important parts of the country, notably Alberta, that are interested in energy development and the pace of development. These are not questions that are seriously addressed here."

Even though White is a senior member of the Press Gallery, known to almost everyone, he has never once been allowed to ask the prime minister a question at a formal news conference in Ottawa. These conferences, held in a theatre in the National Press building on Wellington Street, are run according to an elaborate protocol. This intricate dance of competing interests seems remarkably like the way the country itself is run, right down to the polite but firm shunting aside of the West and the Atlantic region.

An elected Press Gallery official, often the president, sits beside the prime minister or cabinet minister who is holding the news conference. As the reporters file in and take their seats, they raise their hands to catch the eye of the president (this year it's Guy Gendron of the Quebec network TVA). He nods and writes the names on a list, then recognizes each questioner in turn. But the list means very little because the presiding Press Gallery officer has so many needs to consider. First he has to strike a rough balance between French and English questioners. Then he tries to keep parity between print and broadcast media. There are prestigious "national" reporters to consider; finally, he tries to accommodate the "regions," which always means the West and the Atlantic, but might also include local reporters from Toronto and Montreal.

When Mulroney held a news conference at the end of February 1990 (his first in three years and one month), the competition to be recognized was fierce. But almost all the questions for an hour were on the fate of the Meech Lake accord, the big issue of the moment for Quebec reporters as well as the English "national" group. (The one exception was *Globe and Mail* columnist Jeffrey Simpson, who asked about Mulroney's plans for Alberta's Senate nominee.) Mulroney escaped questions about the Prairie farm crisis, the cancellation of the Polar 8 icebreaker project on the West Coast, the virtual collapse of the Atlantic fishery, and many other pressing matters. Bill Rodgers, a reporter with CFTO television in Toronto, says "it wasn't impressive. We'd asked him about Meech Lake a hundred times on the steps [of Parliament] and we got the same answers at the press conference.... After we sat around whining and complaining about not having a press conference for so long, when we got it, we didn't seem to have anything new to ask him....

"A lot of people went away disgusted," says Rodgers,

who is vice-president of the Press Gallery, but emphasizes that he is speaking only for himself. "There's a tendency on the part of Gallery people chairing the meetings to go to the David Haltons ["CBC News"], the Craig Olivers ["CTV News"] and the Jeffrey Simpsons. I suspect they don't always get on the list first, but somebody else gets bumped so they can get their questions in. They're the media stars of the Gallery and they have the big national questions to ask.... With the exception of the French-English factor, which you have to take into account, I would take questions in the order on the list." Rodgers, who calls himself a "regional reporter" from Toronto, was just as frustrated as anyone else; he didn't get a question either.

Only a few days later, there was another graphic illustration of the built-in bias against so-called regional news. Several Prairie MPS, concerned about a new farm crisis, dominated much of the House of Commons question period with their concerns. This was a hot issue in Saskatchewan, where Premier Devine had just announced $250 million in budget cuts to pay for aid to farmers. But there wasn't much excitement in the reporters' gallery above the chamber. A journalist from the *Journal de Montréal* yawned ostentatiously, and later, outside the Commons, a few TV correspondents agreed that there hadn't been any news worth reporting. They were only reflecting the views of their editors and most of their readers and viewers in Central Canada. Such things happen almost every day.

At times, this casual lack of interest can erupt into media hostility toward the provinces. During the energy-pricing crisis of 1980 and 1981, Lougheed faced some remarkably nasty and aggressive news conferences in Ottawa. Many reporters simply assumed that the federal government was right and Alberta was wrong, and the bias showed in their questions. Lougheed believes he knows the reason. "I've always felt that the Ottawa media really had a very strong self-interest in a dominant central goverment," he argues. "The more dominant the government, the more important their position as journalists. If the provinces became stronger, then they had to share that with journalists in other parts of Canada. And so there was a very natural instinctive bias against the provinces through that whole period."

Lougheed thought he saw more evidence during the constitutional debate in 1981. The provinces that lined up against the federal government were tagged "the gang of eight," and Ottawa reporters happily stuck this label on them day after day. When agreement finally came on November 5, the story quickly spread that the impasse was broken during a "kitchen meeting" with Jean Chrétien, Roy Romanow and Ontario's Roy McMurtry. Lougheed had a very different view; the real problems were solved, he says, by three meetings between groups of premiers and a phone call to the prime minister. The kitchen meeting was only part of a much larger picture. Indeed, it has always seemed ridiculous that three ministers would have so much clout when all the government leaders were on the scene. "But the media didn't want that to be the story in Ottawa," Lougheed charges. "And today their story is the conventional wisdom about what happened." (Romanow still insists that the kitchen group played a vital role as "facilitator," because the three ministers could speak to premiers who weren't necessarily speaking to each other.)

And yet, many Ottawa reporters don't fit the general picture painted by Lougheed. The *Globe*'s Simpson is almost fanatical about leaving the capital to learn the truth about Canada. "The country is so damn big," he says, "that paradoxically the only way you can cover the federal government is to get out of Ottawa as often as possible. I find it absolutely indispensable. But a majority of people just sit in Ottawa. I reject that; I think it's absolutely the wrong thing to do." Simpson probably logs more air miles in his pursuit of Canada than any other journalist, but he has rivals in understanding and sensitivity. Michel Vastel, radio commentator and columnist for several Quebec newspapers, has a keen understanding of the West and all English Canada. CTV's Pamela Wallin has never forgotten her Saskatchewan roots depite her rise into the national TV stratosphere. The CBC's Don Newman, as Ottawa host for "Newsworld," conducts shrewd and detailed interviews on regional issues. Marjorie Nichols, despite a serious bout with cancer, still explains the government and the country to her Ottawa readers with amazing energy. Southam News columnist Don McGillivray, a prairie boy who spent many years in Montreal, brings a western populist spirit to his writing.

Canada's political reporters are like politicians though. Some of the best won't go to Ottawa on a bet. Allan Fotheringham has made a career of refusing to be based in the city of "silly servants." Provincial capitals hold some fine columnists who ignore all the flattery and ruses their editors employ to ship them to Ottawa. They include Vaughn Palmer of the *Vancouver Sun*; Dale Eisler of the *Saskatoon Star-Phoenix* and *Regina Leader-Post*; the Montreal *Gazette*'s Don Macpherson in Quebec City; and Thomas Walkom of the *Toronto Star*. Eisler, like most of the others, has had many chances to serve in Ottawa, but he always refuses. "I think that provincial politics, in Saskatchewan particularly, is more important to the people," he says. "I want to write about the things people care about. In Ottawa, issues that are important to us get swallowed up."

Eisler hits the main point: the regions tend to be chewed and swallowed in the capital. The intense frustration of regional MPs of all parties shows this, and so does the narrow focus of so many Ottawa journalists. Only the best of both breeds manage to keep explaining and fighting for their causes without losing heart. What they need – what the whole country needs – is one body in Ottawa where all the regions would have real power and influence. If the Senate were truly effective, reporters couldn't ignore Saskatchewan farm woes, because the Prairie senators might decide to get uppity and hold up bills or block the prime minister's will in some crucial area. This sort of horse-trading goes on in Washington all the time. It turns regional stories into national ones overnight, keeps the central bureaucrats alert, and, ultimately, helps bind the nation together. In a federal system that really works, power belongs in the federal capital. Canada, the unfinished federation, lacks such simple tools for integration and survival.

One of Ottawa's biggest problems is that Canada's brightest provincial politicians don't want to work there. The best provincial leaders dive for cover like jackrabbits when they're approached to run for the leadership of their national parties – Lougheed, Saskatchewan NDP leader Roy Romanow, current Ontario leader David Peterson. The premiers who decide to go over the wall never seem to fulfil their promise. Robert Stanfield, who had been Nova Scotia's premier, never became prime minister; Gerald Regan, a veteran of the same provincial job, was a middling Liberal minister; Dave Barrett, the ex-premier of B.C., failed in his 1989 run for the leadership of the NDP. There is little mutual love or attraction between Canada's senior levels of politics and government

As Roger Gibbons explains, a move from provincial office to Ottawa can actually bring a loss of status. Lougheed expressed this best when he said, only half-jokingly, "Why should I be prime minister of Canada when I already run Alberta?" He felt he would betray the trust of the provincial voters if he left in mid-term to take federal office. He suspected this would ruin his party, and he might have been right. In 1989, Saskatchewan's Romanow must have been asking himself a similar question when he was approached to run for the national NDP leadership: Why be an Opposition leader in Ottawa when he had every chance to be a premier? Especially for westerners, a career in federal politics often brings nothing but trouble back home, while a life in provincial politics can lead to a large measure of respect or even heroic status. When Lougheed battled Ottawa he was like a medieval knight charging the dragon with the whole village behind him. Seventy-five of the province's seventy-nine ridings were held by loyal Tories, and the opinion polls often showed his support at almost 70 per cent.

Statistics reveal an astoundingly low rate of movement between the federal and provincial levels of government. Political scientist Donald Smiley found that in 1974 only 5.3 per cent of Canada's 565 provincial legislators had run in federal elections, and a mere 2.1 per cent of them won. At the same time, just 13.1 per cent of the country's 264 MPs had ever competed in provincial elections, 4.9 per cent successfully. The percentages were little changed in 1980, and there's no sign that they've risen since. The rate of exchange was lowest of all among provincial and federal Liberals, the national governing party during this period.

As a result, there is little shared experience and less understanding between provincial and federal politicians. They come at each other from different worlds and alien political cultures, without even the link of shared goals. Peter Elzinga, a Tory MP for twelve years, who in 1986 made the rare decision to switch to provincial politics, found himself at sea for months as a minister in the Alberta legislature. "In Ottawa it's very confrontational," he says. "There's perhaps too much showmanship. For the first while in the Alberta legislature people found me too aggressive, perhaps rude. But after I got used to it, I began to prefer the more polite atmosphere." Elzinga also had to overcome hostility from provincial Tories who felt he was a federal hotshot lusting to take over. After settling in, though, he had no desire to go back to Ottawa. Ten years in Opposition, and two years as a Government back-bencher with no hope of a cabinet job (his riding was between Don Mazankowski's and Joe Clark's), left him frustrated with federal politics.

In the United States, state politicians don't just seek federal office, they fight for it. They all long to be president, but, failing that, they'll settle for a seat in the Senate. Gibbons notes that "the Senate offers power, prestige and career security in measures unequalled by elected federal positions in Canada." State governors often consider their job a springboard to national office and nobody holds this against them. Their ambition forces them not to burn bridges with the federal politicians they hope to join some day. Gibbons describes the results of this for both countries: "The career aspirations that have strengthened the Senate have thus also strengthened the national governments vis-à-vis the states. In Canada, the opportunity structure provides no such check on the drive for autonomy, and provincial politicians lead the fight to reduce the nation's powers and aggrandize their own."

There's no guarantee, of course, that an elected Senate would carry all the same benefits in Canada. Our large provinces, with their control of resources and municipalities, will always have formidable premiers. But the Senate would certainly divert some of their power to Ottawa, and where power goes, some of our provincial politicians are sure to follow. The mere hint of shared ambition might do wonders for federal-provincial friendship. Under the current system, the lack of such bonds accelerates the drift to breakup.

CONCLUSION

Outsiders Looking In

WESTERNERS WANT ONLY ONE SMALL THING FROM Canada – equality. They long to be equal partners in a truly united land that includes Quebec, pleases the Maritimes and deals fairly with all provinces. Despite the intermittent rage of separatism, the hostility over language, the resentment toward Ontario and Quebec, and the rise of the Reform Party, regional equality is the one basic demand of most westerners. Granting it would go a long way toward easing all the other problems, which are merely symptoms of the larger one. Equality is a small demand to make, surely, of a country that calls itself democratic and fair-minded.

And yet, our lopsided system is so entrenched that the most powerful forces in the country won't even admit that inequality exists. Ontario premier David Peterson has suggested that Prince Edward Island should not have as many Senate seats as Ontario. P.E.I. has so few people, after all –

only 130,600, compared to 9,667,600 in Ontario, at the beginning of 1990. Like many Ontarians before him, Peterson misses the whole point. P.E.I. needs Senate equality *because* its population is so small. Its small band of four MPs is hardly likely to overwhelm Ontario's army of ninety-nine in the federal Parliament. Virtually powerless in the House of Commons, its citizens have little protection against unfriendly federal policies. They are forced to rely on Ottawa's generosity, an uncertain thing at best. Why then is Ontario worried by the thought of P.E.I., with its full provincial status, having an equal voice at one level of government? Does Canada's mightiest province really fear that the tiniest will plunder Ontario's resources, steal its industry, end its economic dominance? Surely not. To people in smaller provinces, Ontario's resistance reveals a fierce, unbending desire to dominate the country for all time. The only other explanation is an insensitivity so deep it numbs the mind. The true answer, one suspects, is a combination of both, mixed with Ontario's complacent belief that it really does speak for all English Canada.

The most vivid expression of this Ontario attitude, perhaps, came in an article printed in the *Globe and Mail* in early 1990 by Joseph Eliot Magnet, a specialist in constitutional law and minority rights at the University of Ottawa law faculty. Writing about the opposition of Manitoba and Newfoundland to the Meech Lake accord, Professor Magnet stated: "Two pip-squeak provinces representing less than five per cent of Canadians, going back on their signatures, will ruin Meech Lake and imperil the noble Canadian experiment." This is an odd view, in light of the very first sentence of Meech Lake, which said the agreement "would recognize the principle of equality of all the provinces" (even the pip-squeaks). The Central Canadian authorities, as usual, presume they hold the keys to the "noble Canadian experiment," when all they speak for is their own opinion.

And their love of minority rights obviously doesn't extend to small provinces with a minority of the population.

California, with nearly thirty million people, does not pretend to wield such power over Alaska, which has fewer than one million. Both send two senators to Washington. New York, with twenty million, doesn't try to strip senators from Rhode Island, with its one million souls. The United States, with its deep sense of national pride implanted in all the states, is a powerful argument for regional equality. America works well as a federal nation, whatever one might think of its foreign policies and social problems. But the example is lost on most Central Canadian leaders. Mention it and they have a series of easy rebuttals. "Oh, our provinces are too big.... There aren't enough of them.... That's the American way, not ours.... You can't transplant an elected senate to a British parliamentary democracy."

These are excuses, not answers, and every one is bogus. Australia grafted such a Senate to the British system nearly ninety years ago. There are only six states; the largest, New South Wales, has nearly six million people; the smallest, Tasmania, has fewer than half a million. Somehow, Australia doesn't collapse under this terrible burden of regional equality. Its states and parties still squabble, but Australia is a far more united country than Canada, with a deeper sense of national identity. Australians have succeeded in nationalizing a diverse country that covers a whole continent; Canadians have only managed to regionalize theirs.

Until quite recently, though, the idea of Senate reform was regarded in Ottawa as a crackpot issue – a "rural eccentricity," in Gordon Robertson's striking phrase. To some politicians and mandarins it still is. They believe they can make the country work with the proper combination of goodwill, good works and legislative tinkering. When the federal Tories took power in 1984, bubbling with lust for "national reconciliation," these ideas propelled them with missionary zeal. A government with 211 seats from all parts of the country could surely please everyone, they thought. The delusion lasted for about two years before regional brawls began to pummel them bloody. After six years, even the sunniest Conservative had to admit that the nation had almost come unglued. Goodwill isn't enough to govern this country. Neither is generosity. Pierre Trudeau could have told the Conservatives that much (although he didn't always demonstrate much of either). The tensions are too powerful to be reconciled by any government, however generous. Ultimately, when regions divide, our leaders always pull back to defend their bases in the provinces with the most seats. This discredits government MPs from the provinces that lose out, creates yet another image of Central Canada against the rest of the country, and helps divide us further. Only a saint could resist this temptation to pull back to the power centres, and Canada has never been run by saints.

The smaller provinces do not need any more of the temporary goodwill that can vanish as quickly as the sun slips behind a cloud. This is a kind of political welfare that creates only dependency and resentment. What the provinces need are the tools to fight for themselves, at the centre of power, on an equal regional footing – the tools of self-respect. The obvious first step is an equal, elected, and effective Senate. Properly built, it would help replace strict party discipline with a measure of old-fashioned horse-trading, a useful western art. If the prime minister wants Ottawa to help pay for a new car plant in Ontario, he should have to submit the enabling bill to a Senate with real authority. A majority of Senators might say, "Sure, you can have that, but next up is the Polar 8 icebreaker in British Columbia, or the fixed link from Prince Edward Island to the mainland. Forget us and you won't get another vote for years." A National Energy Program would have to be modified before it could pass. A better policy would result, and regional anger would diminish. The prime minister and the cabinet would no longer take the full rap for every decision, and even a leader like Mulroney might begin to hear a cheer or two in the smaller provinces. This is how the United States divides regional development, placates regional emotion, and holds the president above the messiest parts of the domestic fray. Government projects and private developments are spread over many states because of horse-trading in the Senate. Even when a state loses a battle, its residents always know two things: the system wasn't hopelessly stacked against them, and somebody will need their Senate votes another day. This method isn't perfect, but it certainly works better than the inequity that prevails in Canada.

Long-standing objections from Ontario appear not only selfish but short-sighted, because in the long run the biggest province would probably benefit most from regional equality. The western premiers whose bleating annoys Ontarians would have their guns spiked by senators doing the regional job properly in Ottawa. The capital, an Ontario city after all, would enjoy even more prestige and authority as the real site of central government. With more action in Ottawa and less in the provincial capitals, Toronto would cement its role as the media centre of English-speaking Canada. Ontario would still be the logical site for the auto industry and many corporate headquarters. And as the smaller provinces began to develop more evenly, the market for Ontario products would grow too. Most of all, Ontario would still have the most seats in the House of Commons, and thus enjoy the most overall influence (which it deserves, having the most people). Westerners should have no illusions about this; an American in Idaho might feel roughly equal to a Californian, but she still knows who carries the hammer in the House of Representatives. Similarly, an elected Senate will never give a farmer in Prince Edward Island the same regional influence as a stockbroker on Bay Street. But the Islander would at last make his voice heard.

The Canadian nationalists who believe Senate reform is a plot for diluting central authority are exactly wrong. A Triple E Senate is really a centralizing device, a way of refederating the country with more authority in the national government. The benefit to the small provinces, of course, is that they would have equal clout in one level of that authority. This is the essence of real federalism in large countries like Canada, the United States and Australia. The big centres might lose a struggle once in a while, but that's the nature of the game. As political scientist Roger Gibbons notes, true federalism forces a few defeats on the population centres. They can fight, and mostly they will win because of their larger representation in one chamber. But they can no longer control every outcome through majority rule, or arrogantly assume the role of paternal gift-giver. A nationalist who can't see the justice in this is really an apologist for dictatorship by numbers.

Quebec's fears about Senate reform are easier to understand and much more valid. Quebecers fear that a Triple E Senate would make them merely one of ten, not distinct at all, subject to one defeat after another on vital issues of cultural survival. The whole notion of provincial equality, in fact, raises the deepest Quebec fears of being swamped by the rest of Canada. This is why the equality provision in Meech Lake always seemed so odd and contradictory beside the distinct society clause. The best proposals on Senate reform all recognize these Quebec concerns and address them. The Alberta report on the Senate, for instance, suggests that all changes affecting French and English should be subject to a double majority veto. This means that a majority of all senators, combined with a majority of francophone senators, could stop any such bill. An even better proposal might be to allow a simple majority of the French speakers to approve or reject any language law affecting Quebec. If movement toward Triple E began in earnest, Quebec might be surprised at how accommodating westerners would be.

After all, Quebec and the West have been silent partners throughout much of Confederation. René Lévesque and Peter Lougheed forged an alliance based on mutual respect and provincial understanding. Lévesque well understood what the loss of resource control meant for Quebec's autonomy. Today Robert Bourassa and the four western premiers share a hidden trust that surfaces whenever Ottawa challenges provincial controls. In the spring of 1990, for instance, Quebec Communications Minister Liza Frulla-Hébert brought the twenty-year Quebec-Ottawa battle for control over communications to the West. She wasn't there to tap the lines of the west's provincially owned telephone networks. Frulla-Hébert wanted western support for a series of provincial telecommunications guidelines that federal minister Marcel Masse couldn't ignore.

Quebec-West support over telecommunications is only the latest in a series of bonds these two solitudes have created. Bureaucrats from both areas consult each other on mutual matters involving Ottawa wresting power from the provinces. These alliances are based on a collective quest for equality. Most westerners have never wanted to thwart Quebec's desires; they are simply angry at having their own ignored for so long, while Quebec's get most of the attention.

Westerners have come to these views slowly, painfully, after many years of agonizing over their role in the country. Often they were accused of being disloyal, even un-Canadian, for disputing the official view of the country. Some feel as guilty as a cleric with lewd thoughts for harbouring feelings that seem to threaten national unity. Official history is powerful and daunting; it holds that only one difference in Canada counts, the one between French and English. Quebecers clutch this opinion almost blindly, admitting to no meaningful variation within "English Canada." This popular Quebec belief is also a useful official position, because it always carries Quebec's grievances above any in the rest of Canada. The Quebec view influences policy makers in Ontario, who know better, but happily agree because it nicely fits their self-image as keepers of the national flame, English version. Federal leaders agree because they don't have the courage to reach for a vision of the whole country; Joe Clark and John Diefenbaker were crushed when they tried. The only bow to other differences is a patronage-ridden multiculturalism that now divides rather than unites. We are locked in an archaic notion of Canada that rings false to almost every western ear. Yet when westerners say what seems true to them, they are branded with all the old labels: crackpot, bigot, nation-wrecker.

John Foster, a brilliant University of Alberta historian, notes that whole generations of westerners know nothing of Central Canada. They came directly to the West from other lands, never visit Ontario or Quebec, and see Canada only through western eyes. Quebec is a mythical land off to the East, and Ontario is merely a name stamped on the back of half the things they buy. "These people include British ranchers, American cowboys, Highland Scots, Ulster Irish, Ukrainians, Germans and many others," Foster says. "They have no family ties whatever in Central Canada." When tensions rise, Foster adds, such people are the most likely to become separatists. The official vision of Canada sends them one powerful message – they aren't included.

Yet there are western pioneers alive today who did as much to build Canada as any *habitant* in eighteenth-century Quebec, or any Englishman in nineteenth-century Ontario. They created the parts of modern Canada that were forged in the early twentieth century – the frontiers of the West. Indians and Métis often helped them clear the land and start their farms. (The contribution of the Native people is almost forgotten today, even by westerners, but many regions could not have been opened to farming without their help.) Many of their original houses still stand today from the farms around Winnipeg to the valleys of the British Columbia interior. All these groups – Natives, Ukrainians, Scandinavians, Germans, even the British who came West – ask the same questions: "Aren't we founders, too? What about *our* Canada? Who speaks for it? Why do we always hear of anglophone and francophone? What kind of country is this that tells me a language I never hear is more important than the one my parents speak?"

To the keepers of official history, these voices flirt with bigotry. They threaten the national myth of duality, so they must be silenced. Prime Minister Mulroney, with typical Quebec testiness, is forever flaring up at such signs of "intolerance." But these voices rise from anger, hurt and confusion, not usually from hatred (although some do). They are the voices of outsiders flailing at a system that consigns them to a secondary place in Canada. If westerners had full political rights in Canada, the French in the West might find themselves getting fairer treatment. Mature citizens can afford to be generous. It's the deprived who resort to meanness.

This would certainly be welcome to western francophones, often the chief victims of regional anger and bitterness. The West isn't free of pettiness or instinct for revenge, and western French speakers often find themselves paying, politically and socially, for ancient grudges against Quebec. Yet Quebec has abandoned them shamefully, as Robert Bourassa's language pact with the western leaders showed very clearly. Neither anglo nor ethnic, with few allies in western provincial governments, little protection from Ottawa, and no help at all from Quebec, western francophones are adrift without anchors, forced to assimilate or fall back on their withering communities. This trend is certain to accelerate as the country retreats deeper into its language ghettos. It's hard to imagine a sadder fate for the proud, brave people who first opened the West to homesteading as missionaries and explorers. If the country hadn't gone so badly awry, if westerners felt more equal and less threatened, the francophones might enjoy the dignity and respect they deserve. Instead, they are just as often told to "go back to Quebec", even though their families might have been in the West for five or six generations.

Westerners always know what they think, but often they know surprisingly little about the real history of their region. John Foster once got a powerful shock when he tried to change the way Alberta high schools teach history. Sitting on a committee to revise the curriculum, he suggested that textbooks be written from a western viewpoint, with less emphasis on two founding races, the deification of John A. Macdonald, and all the old standards of Canadian history. He was turned down flat by the other members, all westerners. They didn't have the nerve to challenge the powerful tenets of "national history," the meat-and-potatoes fare of English-Canadian schools for more than half a century, even though most of them must have felt the tension between this history and their own view of the world.

In the schools, the result of this tension is curious and destructive. Young westerners learn one view of Canada in the classroom, but hear another at home, in the street, at the corner store. In school, they learn that Canada is a compact of the two founding races. At home, the Ukrainian kid listens to his mom and dad say his people are first Canadians, too, because they opened whole regions of Canada. In school, they hear that English and French are the official languages. But in many western schools, the lesson might be taught in Ukrainian or German. In the classroom, they hear that Canada is a great nation of equal citizens from sea to shining sea. Yet their parents, their friends and even the premier of their province might complain every day that Ontario and Quebec run everything.

Because of this dissonance, Foster notes, "many westerners don't believe in formal history. They subscribe rather to folk history, beer-parlour history, the kind of history that is concerned with image. There's a clear division between western folk history and formal history, and when that happens, folk history always wins." It can be accurate and is often useful, he maintains, because it helps people explain and identify themselves within the country.

The main lessons of folk history are similar across the West. Ottawa can't be trusted. Your best friend, if you send him to Ottawa as an MP, can't be trusted. The prime minister might seem friendly for a while, but Ontario or Quebec will always yank his leash before he gets carried away. Official bilingualism is an expensive policy that matters only to Quebec and Ontario. Quebec and its eternal worries are more important to Ottawa than all four western provinces together. Western complaints, especially about language and the Constitution, are dismissed as intolerant. Ontario wants cheap western resources and all the industrial growth for itself. Ottawa makes sure this happens, and placates the West with handouts that don't begin to compensate for the wealth sucked out of the region for a hundred years. Grant Notley, the late leader of the Alberta NDP, caught the profound sense of distance and alienation when he said: "Ottawa is three thousand miles from Alberta, Alberta is three million miles from Ottawa."

There's an element of truth in every one of these beliefs, but they're often stated with no sense of nuance because westerners lack knowledge of their past. Students on the Prairies still learn, from texts printed in Ontario, that Louis Riel was a rebel whose chief benefit to Canada was to bring the Mounties to the West and consolidate the frontier.

There's no mention of the vital fact that some of the things Riel demanded are still valid western grievances today. The crucial matter of resource control is largely ignored, and so is most history of the Progressives, Social Credit, the CCF, the United Farmers, and other movements that arose to do battle with Ottawa. If the history doesn't concern the national Tories and Grits, it probably won't be in the text. Western children might learn of these things, but only if their teacher is energetic and knowledgeable enough to go beyond the textbook.

The culprit here is the economics of school-text production and sales. The big companies, all in Toronto, want to sell their books right across the country. This almost forces them to stick to "national history," because a chapter on, say, the CCF in Saskatchewan might lose them sales in Ontario or the Maritimes. This leaves the old myths: English and French build Canada together, the railroad binds a happy nation, Macdonald rescues the West from grasping Americans. Ontario students get their regional history because so much of it is officially endorsed as national history. But children in the so-called regions can be left in woeful ignorance of their heritage, and that, of course, has its own charm for the keepers of the myth.

Today the genie is out of the bottle. Westerners have a new sense of purpose, a passionate desire to win their way into Canada at last. Senate reform has quickly become one weapon. Others are the region's growing sophistication and expanding economic base. If the rest of Canada can recognize these facts and somehow accept the West on equal terms at last, Wilfrid Laurier will be right, although a century late – the twenty-first century will belong to Canada. But if the West is ignored yet again, left to fester and stew, this country will forever be a mere shadow of its potential, and ultimately no country at all. The test for Canada is this: do Ontario, Quebec and Ottawa have the courage to give up some small part of their control for a far greater good, a truly united Canada?

The choice is theirs. Westerners can only knock at the door and wait, outsiders looking in, hoping that others stop the drift toward breakup.

Index